Meron Zeleke

The Mother and the Bread Winner

Spektrum

Berlin Series on Society, Economy and Politics in Developing Countries

edited by

PD Dr. Dr. Ulrich van der Heyden
Prof. Dr. Volker Lühr
PD Dr. Ulrike Schultz
Prof. Dr. Manfred Schulz

Volume 103

LIT

Meron Zeleke

The Mother and the Bread Winner

The Socio-Economic Role and Status of Gumuz Women

LIT

Coverphoto: Meron Zeleke

Bibliographic information published by the Deutsche Nationalbibliothek
The Deutsche Nationalbibliothek lists this publication in the Deutsche Nationalbibliografie; detailed bibliographic data are available in the Internet at http://dnb.d-nb.de.

ISBN 978-3-8258-1982-8

A catalogue record for this book is available from the British Library

Fresnostr. 2 D-48159 Münster
Tel. +49 (0) 2 51-620 320 Fax +49 (0) 2 51-922 60 99
e-Mail: lit@lit-verlag.de http://www.lit-verlag.de

Distribution:
In Germany: LIT Verlag Fresnostr. 2, D-48159 Münster
Tel. +49 (0) 2 51-620 32 22, Fax +49 (0) 2 51-922 60 99, e-Mail: vertrieb@lit-verlag.de
In Austria: Medienlogistik Pichler-ÖBZ, e-mail: mlo@medien-logistik.at
In Switzerland: B + M Buch- und Medienvertrieb, e-mail: order@buch-medien.ch

In the UK: Global Book Marketing, e-mail: mo@centralbooks.com

In North America by:

Transaction Publishers
New Brunswick (U.S.A.) and London (U.K.)

Transaction Publishers
Rutgers University
35 Berrue Circle
Piscataway, NJ 08854

Phone: +1 (732) 445 - 2280
Fax: + 1 (732) 445 - 3138
for orders (U. S. only):
toll free (888) 999 - 6778
e-mail: orders@transactionpub.com

ACKNOWLEDGMENT

My heartfelt thanks go to my family: *Ato* Tefera Dheressa and *Weizero* Kelemwa Mengesha, *Weizero* Roman Tefera, Dr Zeleke Eresso, Tekle Dheressa, Mesfin Tefra, Haile and Tiruwerik Tesfaye. I would like to thank my husband Dr. Dereje Feyissa for the discussions we had and for his constructive comments and for his ongoing support in my academic carrier.

I would like to thank my friend Selamwit Mekonnen who was with me at different levels of my study since high school for her encouragement and moral support. My friends Penelope Sardone and Wegayehu Negassa are among those whom I would like to acknowledge for their encouragement, support and friendship during my study. I would like to thank Fitsum Yohannes for accompanying me during my stay in the field and the support he offered in various ways. I gratefully acknowledge CPAR (Canadian Physicians for Aid and relief) who provided me with financial support to carryout the field work. Last but not least, I would like to thank my informants for it is their story that contributed to this work.

Dedication

This Book is dedicated to my grandfather Ato Tefera Dheressa.

TABLE OF CONTENT

CHAPTER 1

INTRODUCTION

Women contribute a lot to a society as mothers, wives and workers (Tsehai 1991). However, this contribution of women was overlooked by scholars or remained invisible until 1970, the time when the book by Ester Boserup *Women's Role in Economic Development* was published (Moser 1994; Keessing 1981). It was following her work that the United Nation's Decade for women (1976-1986) was declared along with different policy approaches to the third world which encouraged women to work on gender and developmental issues (Moser 1998). As Moore (1988: 44) highlights this fact,"Boserup's book is an important starting point because it raises issues which have dominated discussion on women's status and economic roles in society, and which have subsequently inspired much of the empirical work conducted over the last decades".

This pioneering work by Boserup has come up with a model, which has been referred to by many scholars. According to Boserup's model, among the sparsely populated hoe-based agricultural societies in Africa, women are responsible for most of the agricultural activities and among the densely populated plough agriculturalist societies women contribute relatively smaller share. Goody (1976) also observes the correlation between the type of agricultural technology and women's contribution to agricultural production. In other words, their argument is that the farming technology is a factor that accounts for the gender-based division of labor in a society. Goody (1976) explains that in Eurasia where plough agriculture dominates male farming is the norm, while in Africa where hoe agriculture dominates; female farming is the common pattern.

Besides, they both assert that in hoe-based agricultural communities, polygamy is a common practice where at the same time marriage by bride wealth payment is the rule. Goody (1976: 34) advances a similar position, as monogamy is most likely to be found with male farming while polygamy is the predominant form among the female farming. In a nutshell this model was postulated as follows: hoe based agricultural technology → dominated by women performing most agricultural activities → polygamous marriage being the dominant form of marriage → marriage by bride wealth payment is the rule. This, according to Boserup (1970) and Goody (1976), holds true for all African agricultural societies whose life is based on shifting cultivation. Boserup (1970) pushes the correlation further to the issue of access to fruits of labour, and she asserts that women in those shifting cultivating societies enjoy freedom of movement, right of disposing fruits of their labour, and decision making right on spending the income to be earned. Thus on top of Goody's postulation Boserup added a new dimension in the nexus between agricultural technology and principles of social organization, i.e., greater empowerment of women in decision making.

There are numerous literatures on the gender based division of labour (Bossen 1980, Boserup 1970, Goody 1976, Rogers 1980, Szalai, 1975, Tinker 1990). Several books and articles have been written on the Gumuz society (James 1977, 1986; Wallmark 1981; Tadesse; 1988; Irwin 1968). Besides, scores of BA and MA theses are written on different aspects of Gumuz society such as Edossa (1982); Damie (1980); Emiru (1984),and Abeyya (2001). There are important works on Gumuz, living in Metekel zone close to the study area; Tefera (1986); Waldeselassie (2002); Desalagn(1988) and Berihun (1996,2004). These studies deal hardly with gender except in the few instances where they tend to touch upon issues related to women without thoroughly analyzing women's socioeconomic role and status.

Almost all of the existing literatures pertaining to the Gumuz do not go beyond giving descriptions of some cultural practices and the productive system in which women's role in the society is only sparingly touched upon. Thus, the issue of the correlation between the existing modes of agriculture and women empowerment (the correlation between type of production, the socioeconomic gender role, type of marriage and the socioeconomic status of women in the society) is a topic that calls for a comparative research work.

The study is conducted on the socio economic role and status of Gumuz women. It examines the interplay among the variables mentioned above (type of production technology, the gender role in production, marriage pattern and socioeconomic status of women) through a case study of Gumuz society, a society in Northwestern Ethiopia that makes its living on shifting cultivation. Moreover, it addresses the socioeconomic status of women among the Gumuz by giving due emphasis on their access to resources and their rights in decision making on fruits of their labour and in different social, economic and political matters in the community.

RESEARCH METHODS

Different sources of data and data collection methods are employed. To materialize the objective of the study an exclusive qualitative method of data collection was implemented. The primary sources of data used in this material mainly include those collected through personal in-depth interview, case histories, focus group discussions (FGDs) and participant observation methods.

Field data collection tools such as field note taking, tape recording and photographing were used.

IN-DEPTH INTERVIEW

Personal in-depth interview was used in collecting empirical data. The interview was conducted with young girls, women, and men from the Gumuz society on issues relating to their socio- economic role and their right of owning property and making decision on different issues at the household and community level. Unstructured interviews were conducted utilizing a checklist. The interview was conducted in the Gumuz language with the help of the interpreters Habte Kebede and Iyasus Warqe who are both fluent in Gumuz and Amharic languages. This exercise brought to light different issues in the everyday lives of women and their experiences.

FOCUS GROUP DISCUSSIONS (FGDS)

Group discussions were conducted with members of the community representing people of different age and sex groups. Those participants of the FGDs were people from different walks of life. This was done with the purpose of acquiring valid data on issues that need group idea and consensus. Three focus group discussions were held. The first group discussion consisted of six men from two different clans. The focus group discussion was held at a *kiya* ceremony (which is a party held for a labour commune mobilized for different activities) where the men were gathered at the place of Bele Bakare, from *Dabasa* clan in Dabasa village. The arrangement was made in a way that three persons from each of the two dominant clans *(*Dabasa and Dibishwua*)* in the study villages could be enrolled. The topics for the focus group discussion were mainly on issues dealing with the role of women in the society, the existing pattern of marriage, the right of women to own and use resources and their decision making rights in the society and factors shaping gender role, marriage pattern and the socioeconomic status of women in the society. The Discussion with the group of men has helped to analyze the dominant gender ideology existing in the community as to be discussed in details in the following chapters.

Another group discussion was held with a group of six women in the same village who were from different clans and who came to the area through exchange marriage. These women were from the clans known as Dibudiya, Yidangla, Jipqaya, Daghohiya, Dibishwua and Dibaymasa. The selection of informants from different sex and clan was meant to find out if there are any different views across clan boundaries among the Gumuz and to bring forward matters pertaining to the socioeconomic role and status of women and to get detailed data on the issue of concern in the study. The third focus group discussion was conducted with six young unmarried girls from Dabasa and Dibishwua clans from Dabasa and *Lay* Moga villages respectively. This third discussion was held with the aim of addressing the topics under discussion and to see if there are any generational differences in the way of presenting and reflecting on the topic under discussion.

PERSONAL CASE STUDIES

This has been used to check the veracity of what informants said in the focus group discussions and in-depth interview. The personal accounts of a few informants were used to elaborate the generalized points discussed and raised in the ethnography. And the cases helped to exemplify the generalized issues raised.

PARTICIPANT OBSERVATION

Informal Participant observation was conducted by the writer to add up to the reliability of information gathered on the issues under discussion. Such observation and participation at different social events has raised additional research questions appealing from the observation of some events. These social events include participating at a *kiya* (local beer) drinking ceremony usually held for a labor exchange. The daily routines of Gumuz woman were observed by spending days with different women. I have got the chance to participate in a workshop at Dibatie town on gender and women empowerment in the society, organized by CPAR. Purposeful and systematic observation of some events was made to get relevant information on the subject under study.

For the purpose of analysis and enriching the discussion, secondary sources of published and unpublished materials were consulted that are clearly cited and acknowledged in the reference. The relevant secondary sources were used to formulate the problem, to supplement the ethnographic description and in the summary part. Besides, data were collected from different governmental, non-governmental, and private institutions. These include statistical data from different *wereda* offices such as the agricultural bureau and the *wereda* health department.

THE SCOPE OF THE STUDY

The scope of the study is limited to the issue of the socio economic status and role of Gumuz women in one of the three zones, the Metekel zone of Benishangul regional state. As the different zones differ in cultural practices regarding the same issues under discussion, it is difficult to say the discussions in this text holds true for the Gumuz society at large.

The discussions raised in this text might be a valuable addition to the scanty literature on the topic. The findings presented in this material could also contribute to policy formulation. Furthermore, it can be used as a basis for development intervention on issues related to women in the study area.

CHAPTER 2

DEBATING GENDER AND SOCIOECONOMIC EMPOWERMENT

To analyze the ethnographic data some of the literatures on three relevant topics have been reviewed. These topics include: gender-based division of labor, the gender dimension of differential access to resources and decision-making, and the relationship between agricultural technologies; forms of marriage and types of marriage payment.

GENDER BASED DIVISION OF LABOR

The literature reviewed under this subheading mainly deals with the different factors described by different scholars that account for gender-based division of labor. The discussion on the roles assigned to women in different societies with different modes of production, and the debate on the static and rigidity of the gender based labor division pattern were briefly reviewed.

Barbara Rogers (1980) explains the difference between sex and gender, respectively, as biological and cultural (societal) dimensions. Min-ha defines gender as the "eminently local and time bound duality that sets off men and women under circumstances and conditions that prevent them from saying, doing, desiring, or perceiving the same thing" (Min-ha, 1989: 105). Pine(1996: 253) similarly highlights that that the term gender is used to refer to both the male and the female, the cultural construction of these categories, and the relationship between them . Gender refers to the expectations people have from someone because they are female or male.

Regarding gender roles, Rogers points out that, "In talking of the division of labor between men and women in different societies we are talking almost exclusively of gender roles rather than sex roles, determined by culture rather than biology" (Rogers, 1980: 12-13). Hadfield (1999) mentions that this division of labor is a common phenomenon of all societies at all stages of societal development.

Bossen (1989) and Desalagn (1989), highlight the fact that this global phenomenon varies from region to region and from one community to the other. Thus according to Bossen (1989), the division of labor is something that does not have a universal structure but rather a culturally situated meaning. Amott and Matthew (1991: 4) similarly state the difference as"…. each racial/ethnic group has a sexual division of labor which has barred individuals from the activities of the opposite sex". Sandy (1970) states that the activities are defined as domestic and public domains. The domestic ones include those activities related to the family unit while the public domain is related to the political and economic activities, which are said to be dominated by men.

There are some scholars who explained a similarity in gender-based division of labor in different societies of the world. The early work by Mead as quoted by Boserup (1970: 16) is one of those works " the home shared by a man or men and female partners, into which men bring the food and women prepare it, is the basic common picture the world over". Tasks of child bearing and rearing are said to be activities reserved for women and said to have universal similarity. For instance, Beattie (1964), states that the responsibility of working on productive activities to earn income to the family is that of men while activities such as child bearing and rearing are the main tasks that keep women at home. She further describes that besides caring for children activities such as cooking and caring for members of a family are that of women. Similarly, Mair (1965: 54) elaborates this point further as "in every society the division of roles between the sex's results from the fact that women bear and suckle children, and so they are tied to the domestic scene for much of their lives".

Zenebework and Yared (2000: 32) mention that there is a universal similarity on gender based division of labour in some activities like reproduction: "It was found that cross-culturally the gender division of labour in reproductive activities tends to be homogenous".

Andromeda (1968: 13) discusses the issue with respect to Ethiopian women saying: "It goes without saying that the major role of Ethiopian women is the same as that of women everywhere. She is a home maker and she fulfils her major role as a wife and mother". Rogers (1980: 11) similarly states: "It is thought 'natural' that a woman's place is in the home and that she has a very specific set of tasks, which are thought to be universal because they are, based on the biological imperative of sex. The most important role for women defining their entire life is portrayed as "the bearing and bringing up of children". However, it is said that their role goes unnoticed in most cases. Hanna (1990) argues that despite the major roles of women in a society and though they shouldered the household chores, women's function at social, economical, political and administrative level was not considered significant.

FACTORS SHAPING THE GENDERED ROLES

As mentioned above different scholars have tended to show the global similarity in the nature of gender- based division of labor, especially where the productive roles of earning income to the family are said to be the domain of men while women are described as responsible for the child bearing and rearing activities. Different factors are said to account for the patterns of gendered division of labor. Such factors as strength, economic value of products, socialization, size of population and technology of production are some of the factors said to be shaping the gender-based division of labor.

One of the anthropological theories for the gender based division of labor (strength theory) has the basic premises that women tend to perform activities that require lower energy while men are in charge of taking care of arduous and tiresome activities (Bossen, 1989). Such domestic tasks as cooking, grinding and fetching water are said to be that of women and young girls. While those tasks as hunting, weapon making and construction are said to be men's domain (Rogers, 1980).The central idea in the theory is that strength is the major criteria for defining the gender-based division of labor in a given society. Similarly a study conducted by FAO in 1980 has the same premises that men do the heavy intermittent jobs while women perform simple tasks. Tiger, (1969) also states that the physical strength of men enables them to have access to or get involved in some activities exclusively. Thus physical strength is said to be a landmark in the gender-based division of labor, where men are believed to have more strength than women.

Other scholars have raised socialization as a factor shaping the division of labor on the basis of gender. Newman (1997) mentions that socialization determines what it takes to be a man or a woman and what he or she should do and should not do across a range of activities and situations. Kahler (1995) also shares the same view that through socialization people learn skills and knowledge and what to do with regard to the roles assigned on the basis of gender. They both state that socialization at early ages set the gender specific duties to be accomplished at early age and in the future. Tiger (1969) states that besides men being stronger than women they are socialized in such a way as to be involved in some activities related with violence. As Tiger (1969: 86) noted "... male are stronger than female, that they are directly socialized to accept and use violence, that they form the major structure of defense and police in all communities, all generally reflect a genetically programmed behavioral disposition". Thus he points out that such activity as military campaigns are reserved for men.

The third factor considered to shape gender- based division of labor is the point raised by Boserup (1970) and Goody (1976) above. They have tried to draw a correlation between type of agricultural technology and gender -based division of labor. Boserup (1970) gives two factors for the gender role demarcation: size of population and agricultural technology. She argues that in sparsely populated areas of Africa women tend to do most of the agricultural and domestic activities whereas in most populated areas where plough agriculture dominates, it is the men who do most of the farm work. She has described this as: "The sex roles in farming can be briefly described as follows: in very sparsely populated regions where shifting cultivation is used, men do little farm work, the women doing most. In somewhat more densely populated regions, where the agricultural system is that of extensive plough cultivation, women do little farm work and men do much more" (Boserup 1970: 35). The findings of Goody (1976) who used a sample data drawn from different societies fit that of Boserup. He similarly shares the view that the agricultural technology and population size affect gender role.

On the other hand Dixon-Muller (1989) argues that the change in agricultural technology affects the division of labor on a small scale and that women play a very important role in plough agriculture too.

The common observation that women are displaced from agricultural work with the adoption of plough and other forms of intensification of cultivation maybe true of their relative labor contribution, for example, but in absolute terms, women often spend as much time in field work, livestock care, and crops processing in intensive plough societies as they do in hoe system (Dixon-Muller, 1989: 9).

Those studies conducted on the role of women in Africa share the common view that women contribute a lot in the different productive activities irrespective of the different modes of productions. Bryson (1981: 30) states "women in Sub-Saharan Africa have a predominant role in agricultural production". Boserup (1970) elaborates this point explaining that in African agricultural system women perform more hours on work than men:

> Africa is a region of female farming par excellence. In many African tribes, nearly all tasks connected with food production continue to be left to women. In most of these tribal communities, the agricultural system is that of shifting cultivation: small pieces of land are cultivated for a few years only until the natural fertility of the soil diminishes. When that happens, the field is abandoned and another plot is taken under cultivation. Tree felling is always done by men, most often by young boys of 15 to 18 years, but to women fall the subsequent operations: the removal and burning of the felled tress; the sowing or planting in the ashes; the weeding of the crop; the harvesting and carrying in the crop for storing or immediate consumption (Boserup, 1970: 16-17).

Various scholars in Ethiopia (Tiruneh, 1976 and Hanna, 1990) have also discussed that women at different parts of the county have less leisure time than men. Dejene (1989) also discusses that woman's labor is something that is neither confined to the house nor dominant in the field. Zenebewerik (1975: 35) describes the role of women in Ethiopia as "the day begins when the cook crows and that they are the last to go to bed at night".

The role of women is said to differ in different societies with different modes of production. The significant role of women in different modes of production is the other area on which the literature has been reviewed. Scholars have discussed women's contribution among horticultural societies, pastoralist, agro pastoralist societies and agricultural ones. Susan and Mary (1990) mention that among the horticultural societies in addition to the responsibility of caring for children, women are in charge of preparing food for members of the family and participating in food production. Bonvillan (1995) mentions among the horticultural communities of the Yanomamo in Brazil, the productive work is partially left for men while women are busy with childcare and domestic activities. Thus they are said to be involved in both domestic and farm activities. And among these horticultural societies women are the ones having less leisure time.

Bonvillan also cites that among the pastoralist societies of North American plain a woman's contribution in the household activities and tasks of production is very significant. Women participate in both the pastoralist activities of herding cattle and the household tasks of preparing food to all members of a given family. In the case of agro- pastoralist societies of the Nuer in Sudan (Evans-Pritchard 1951) women are responsible for such tasks as milking cattle twice a day, tending gardens, growing millet and maize, caring for children, and domestic activities including food preparation and keeping up the living quarter. Thus in agro pastoralist and pastoralist societies, the role of women in productive activities is very significant.

Among the agriculturalist societies of India women participate in tasks such as food preparation, childcare and other domestic cores. In addition women are involved in agricultural activities such as weeding and harvesting crops and they help in harvesting grains and various vegetables and fruits (Bonvillan 1995).

Similarly, Ethiopian women in societies with differing modes of production have different roles to play. For example, among the agro- pastoralist societies of Tsamako women take part in agricultural activities like hoeing, ploughing, planting, weeding, harvesting, transporting and storing the harvest and marketing. Their pastoralist activities include tasks such as herding stocks, milking cattle and goats, watering stock and feeding them (Melesse, 1994). They are active participants in the production process. Ragassa (2000) explains that among the agriculturalist societies of Maqi Oromo, culture prescribes agricultural tasks for men. Women among the society are confined to household tasks and child bearing. However, widows and women from poor households participate in the agricultural production.

Among the shifting cultivation societies of Ethiopia Waldeselassie summarizes the activities performed by Gumuz women as follows:

> Gumuz women are observed as the most ingenious and hardest working members of the community. They perform innumerable livelihood activities tirelessly. Apart from performing several gender specific home chores and many others, they are

also fully involved at all levels in the field production as well as construction and exchange activities (Waldeselassie, 2002: 94).

The issue of the change and continuity of existing gender based division of labor in a society is an area of contestation for different scholars. Some argue that gender based division of labor in a given society is rigid while others highlight its dynamic and flexible natures.

In those societies, where women have more workload in production, Chaftez (1989) observes that men always want to maintain the trend. In cases where men have more access to resources and decision-making they always want to retain it. In order to save the system men create gender ideology, stereotype and some gender norms. In contrast to Chaftez's view of the static nature of the gender division of labor, Lorber and Susan (1991) describe it as being flexible, which can be reshaped by the society practicing it. They explain that it is rather a changing phenomenon that can be reshaped by women themselves whenever the need for it arises. Rogers (1980) also says "In many societies the division of labor is flexible" (1980: 15).

With respect to issues pertaining to the gender based division of labor this study tries to address the three questions with regard to the Gumuz community: What are the roles of men and women among the Gumuz integral shifting cultivating community? What factors shape this division of labor (Is it strength, socialization, intensity of farming, modes of production, or size of population?) And are these roles considered as changing or are they perceived as static by the society?

DISEMPOWERMENT AND DIFFERENTIAL ACCESS TO MEANS OF PRODUCTION (RESOURCES)

The literature reviewed in this part mainly deals with women's access to resources and decision making power in a society and those factors that shape this socio-economic process.

People gain or lose land and properties being members of social groups through inheritance and/or purchase. Moser (1998) highlights the fact that women in most societies do not have the rights to acquire, administer, control, use and transfer land and other property. Various scholars have noted the fact that African women do not have right over the means of production (Bryceson, 1995).

Njoku (1980; 79), for instance, stated, "African women have no right to land. Their culture does not allow them to dispose of any piece of land, although they could use the land for the production of food, by the virtue of being a wife, sister, daughter, and or cousin". Different scholars (Davison, 1988; Sachs, 1996) share the view that the ownership right and access of women to means and factors of production such as land and education is low and/ or almost non-existent in Africa. In a similar manner Staudt (1995) maintains that despite their contribution to the economy women in most cases are denied of access to property. Their labor contribution in different activities goes unnoticed. He uses the example of Kenya where women are the primary food producers being responsible for 80% of food crop production contributing substantially to cash crop production but owning only 5% of the land.

However, in some societies, especially in matriarchal societies, women have some rights to own, use and inherit land. Keller, et al. (1990) summarize the early anthropological literature for the Bemba, Tonga and Lozi and illustrate how some of women's land could be passed on to their heirs. Bohhanan (1968) discuss how women's land ownership and control rights among the Tiv of Nigeria depend on their right through birth and marriage, where they are said to have access to own and use means of production, specifically land.

Different factors account for the denial of women's access to own resources and to use them. The intensity of agriculture among some African countries is said to be one of the many reasons. According to Bernal the community residing at the village of Wad al Abbas in southern Sudan, women used to have a right to use and inherit land until the introduction of irrigated scheme by the British to the area in 1954. This scheme brought a significant change in the amount of production, which lead to a large-scale modern farming, which yields much more than the previous days. The scheme reduced women's control over land and women were thereafter denied their right of owning, buying and selling, receiving and giving land as alms, which they used to do prior to the introduction of the irrigated scheme. Bernal explains the relationship between the introduction of the irrigation scheme, the change in production technology, economic role of men and women, and the overall effect of the irrigation scheme on the lives of women in the society. With the introduction of the irrigation scheme the traditional farming technology was replaced with modern farming tools, which were dominated by men who were employed in the irrigation project. The economic role of women as a result remained to small-scale production for household consumption.

Nashimiyu as quoted by Davison (1988: 15) explains this point further:

> Since the production of cash and subsistence crops were directly linked to the access of land, women were confronted with a whole range of handicaps in fulfilling their roles as producers. Lack of control over land and all that goes with it becomes a major cause of women's economic dependence. Without land women were reduced to a state of dependency with no security and only provision of labor.

Guyer (1984) and Davison (1988) observed the same link between cash crop production and women's reduced access to and ownership of the land. With the increase in value of the income to be obtained from cash crop production women came to lose their rights to means of production.

> With the advent of colonialism selected crops became commoditized for export production and women's control over all aspects of production and allocation continued for some food crops. For other [crops] that obtained cash value women's control was increasingly limited to allocating labour tasks such as hoeing, weeding, harvesting and processing; men largely pre-empted women's allocations rights over crops grown for a cash value [....] Gender specialization became intensified with men growing many cash crops such as coffee, palm oil, tobacco, sisal, etc, while women continued to produce food crops in large parts of Africa (Davison 1988: 13).

Nelson (1981) states that in cash crop production men always play a very significant role, while women are confined to production for the domestic consumption. Thus, Davison (1988) and Sachs (1996) further argue that there are crops assigned to men and women on the basis of the market value of those crops. Sachs (1996) states that there is a global pattern in gender assignment of crops where crops raised for market are said to be that of men. And those crops like vegetables are said to be that of women.

The other reason said to account for denial of access to resources is the demographic factor. Boserup (1970) and Bryson (1981) explain that women's access to land and their control over it was a common practice at the time when the size of population was lower. According to Boserup (1970) in sparsely populated societies in Africa, women play a very significant role in production activities and they have a right of enjoying fruits of their labour. In her words with the increase in the number of population men start moving to the productive activities and also controlling both the means and fruits of production. The other possibility she mentions in such instances of population increase is "Sometimes the increase in population pressure may induce men to emigrate from the region in search of wage labour elsewhere" (Boserup: 1970: 19).

Njoku (1980) pushes the issue further and suggests that the denial of their access to land results in denial of access to education due to what he describes as the, *'traditional African philosophy of education'* where the book knowledge is a power and such a power should be reserved only for the males who will inherit the land. Thus he bases his argument from different angle in that he says the denial of access to education as having an implication on access to owning land in a vicious circle. Moreover, men are said to control women and their labour contribution in production). Sachs (1996) and Staudt (1995) point that men tend to control women's labour and that policy makers in Africa recognize only the labour contribution of men.

Women's access to land, resources and agricultural labour is limited. This is mainly because these resources like land, women's labour are considered to be naturally men's property (Davison 1988, Rogers 1980, and Sachs 1996).

In addition to their denial of access to resources due to different factors, women are also denied right of decision making on issues pertaining to their family income and expenditure. Bryson (1981;7-8) states "[...] frequently women find themselves working harder but having no greater control over their products or participate in family or community decision making". Moser (1998) raises the point that the proportion of time spent by woman on domestic activities and on the farm has no effect on her decision making in domestic matters.

Nelson (1981) noted that majority of women are denied rights of decision making on issues such as selling livestock and crop. Mohiuddin (1997) substantiates this view by drawing on the experience of Pakistani women. Though women in Pakistan are integral to the Pakistan economy, extensively engaged in the rural and urban economic sector, their contributions go unnoticed and they have lower access to the fruits of their labor and have no right in deciding over it.

This denial of ownership and decision-making rights are said to be factors accounting to their subordinate status and disempowerment in socio-political domains (Bryson, 1981; Davison, 1988 and Sachs, 1995). The experience of Ethiopian women is of no difference. Daniel (1979) highlights the subordinate status of women in northern Ethiopia where the customary law did not allow women to inherit land unless the father died before giving her in marriage, in which case she was entitled to a dowry or in the absence of male issues. The situation is even more compounded in southern Ethiopia where women could not inherit land (Daniel, 1979). Zenebework (1982) and Desalagn (1991) point out that the overall patriarchal system of kinship and the resultant absence of women's access to land contribute to the secondary status that women hold in most societies in the country.

With regard to the issue of differential access to resources and decision making power of women in Gumuz society, this study addresses three basic points, namely: 1) women's access to factors of production and the decision making power of women 2) identifying those factors determining access to means of production and 3) the status of women in Gumuz society.

CORRELATION BETWEEN MODES OF PRODUCTION AND WOMEN EMPOWERMENT

Different scholars have suggested that there is a correlation between types of agricultural technology, gender role in production, marriage pattern and the decision making power of women. To start with the first part of the assumption which addresses the relationship between agricultural technology and gendered division of labor, Desalagn (1989: 5) writes that, "gender based activity has often been the outcome of technology". Similarly Boserup (1970: 35), earlier pointed out that: "in very sparsely populated regions where shifting cultivation is used, men do little farm work, the women doing most..." whereas she explains the opposite being the case with plough based farming technology.

The other part of this assumption, the existence of a relationship between gender role and marriage pattern can be inferred from the earlier anthropological work of Murdock (1960: 37) who explains the relationship between marriage pattern and gender role as follows:

> The division of labor by sex in a particular setting may well determine in considerable measure the preferred form of marriage. Where women make an insignificant contribution to economic life, polyandry becomes a satisfactory adjustment, when the productive accomplishment of the two sexes is approximately equal monogamy may be economically advantageous. When women's economic contribution is large, and a man can produce enough in his sphere to satisfy the needs of several women, polygamy fits the circumstances.

Polygamy is said to be one of the common features of African marriage (UN, 1990). Boserup (1970) and Goody (1976) mention that polygamy is a common practice among African societies where the hoe based farming dominates and where the role of women in the agriculture is higher. In her chapter on the economics of polygamy Boserup (1970: 37) points out that: "[...] a man can get more food if he has more land, and more wives to cultivate it'. She further adds that: "in female farming communities, a man with more than one wife can cultivate more land than a man with only one wife. The institution of polygamy therefore is a significant element in the process of economic development in regions where additional land is available".

Boserup outlined two factors to explain the need for polygamy: the reproductive and productive roles of women: "In regions of shifting cultivation, where women do all or most of the work of growing food crops, the task of felling the tress in preparation of new plot is usually done by younger boys and very young men. "An elderly cultivator with several wives is likely to have several boys who can be used for this purpose" (Boserup, 1970: 38). The need for children again has an economic implication for Boserup, in that the need for having more children is basically associated with the need for additional labor force.

She further discusses that in African communities where women shoulder the burden of food production and domestic activity women welcome additional wives. In such polygamous marriage she describes the status of a junior wife as being equal to a servant; "Normally a status of the younger wife is inferior as befits the assistant or even servant to the first wife" (Boserup, 1970: 45).

Different scholars have similarly suggested that economic benefit is a factor that is calling for polygamy. Martin (1978) explains that where there is an extra land available women do a great share of farm work. Hence, men tend to marry more wives. The need for women's labor in agriculture being a factor calling for polygamy is a point discussed by Bryson (1981) who states that, "Obviously, the predominant role of women in agricultural production is essential to the attractions of polygamy in this regard" (1981: 360). Parkin and Nyamawaya (1978) also write that in Africa men tend to marry more wives to gain wealth by using women's labor for production. All the scholars mentioned above have the same view that the main factor for polygamy is its economic benefit.

Goody (1976) and Boserup (1970) draw a relationship between the farming system and type of marriage payment. Boserup (1970) says that in hoe-based agricultural societies and where polygamy is the common form of marriage, marriage by bride wealth payment is the rule. Boserup, (1970: 50) generalizes the condition among shifting cultivating communities: "In such communities, we can expect to find a high incidence of polygamy, and bride wealth being paid by the future husband or his family". Goody (1976: 7) also affirms the above point, that marriage by bride wealth payment is the rule in hoe-based farming community. The justification given for this by them is that women in such communities due to their productive roles mentioned above are considered as economic assets contributing the highest share in the production activity.

Do these hypotheses hold true for all shifting cultivating society? I will try to analyze the question by taking the case of the Gumuz. Is it the agricultural technology that defines the gender role among the Gumuz? What is the factor that explains the need for polygamy among the Gumuz? Is marriage by bride wealth payment the rule? These are some questions to be addressed in the study.

CHAPTER 3

BACKGROUND TO THE STUDY AREA

LOCATION

Benishangul Gumuz Region is one of the regional states of the Federal Democratic Republic of Ethiopia. It stretches along the Sudanese border between 09.17°and 12.06°N. The western and eastern limits are given by the longitude 34.10° and 37.04° respectively. The region is bounded by national and international boundaries. Benishangul-Gumuz Region is located along the western escarpment of Ethiopia between Gambella Region in the south, the Sudan to the west, and Amhara and Oromiya Regions to the northeast and east.

The region comprises nineteen *weredas*, out of which two (Tongo and Pawe) are special *weredas*. These *weredas* are organized under three zones, namely: Metekel, Assosa and Kamashi. The region's administrative capital, Assosa town, is located 687 kms west of Addis Ababa. Based on recent boundary delineation the area of the region is estimated to be 51,000km^2.

Metekelzone is one of the three zones in the region located in northwestern part of the country. Metekel used to be one of the provinces in Gojjam until 1989 when it was upgraded into the status of administrative zone. The capital of the zone is Giligel Beles, which is situated at 555 kms distance from Addis Ababa in the northwestern direction. According to the 2007 preliminary census result the population o f the region is 670,847. Of this total number the Gumuz are 21.11 % percent of the region's population; the third largest group in the region and the second largest indigenous group after the Berta which constitute 25.9% of the region's population.

Metekelzone has an estimated total area of 22,028-km^2. The altitudes of the zone ranges from 600 meters to 2731 meters above sea level at Belaya Mountain. According to the data of a study by the zone's agricultural department cited by Waldeselassie (2002), Metekel is mostly lowland

(74%), hilly (16%), valley bottoms (6%), and the rest (4%) is a mountainous land. The climatic condition of the zone is classified as: 82% *qolla*, 10% *woinadega* and 8% *dega*. Besides the estimate of the land use pattern indicates that 79% is covered with savannah forestland, 7% cultivated land, 7% cultivable land, and 7% non-utilized land. The type of forest dominating in the study area is mainly savannah woodland. The average annual temperature of the zone according to data from Dibatie *wereda* agricultural office ranges from 17-32°c. There are seven *weredas* in the zone, namely: Dangur, Guba, Dibatie, Bulen, Wenbera, Pawe Special *wereda*, and Mandura.

The study was carried out in Dibatie district, located in Metekel zone. It lies in 10°01-10°53' North latitude and 36°04-36°26 East longitude. Dibatie *wereda* is bordered by Mandura *wereda* in the north, Wambera *wereda* in the west, and Amhara region in the east and Oromiya region in the south. It is also bounded by water bodies such as Dura river in the east, Abbay in the south, Shai River in the west and Mandura River in the North-East.

According to a Situational Analysis and Baseline Information of the *wereda* prepared by CPAR (2000), having the average elevation of 1500-1700 masl, the *wereda* is generally classified as *qolla* agro ecological zone. The average annual rainfall of the *wereda* according to the same source ranges between 900-1300mm.

The wet and rainy seasons are between May and October. The *kebeles* lowest administrative unit has recently been revised and the *wereda* consists of a total of fifteen *kebeles* namely: Dibatie, Yamp, Angtok, Wubgish, Sirban, Parzeyt, Girz, Berber, Donbon, Marartu Lagabuna, Bechati, Gipo, Galesa, Korka, and Albasa.

Angtok *kebele,* the main focal point of this study is a combination of three former *kebeles* called Moga, Menbereselam, and Angtok. It is located to the east of Dibatie town, the capital of the *wereda.* According to the Situational Analysis report of CPAR (2000) the total population of the *kebele* in the year 2000 was 3555, 1885 male and 1670 female. These former *kebeles* are currently *got's (*sub divisions in kebeles*)* in the *kebele*. According to the information obtained from the *wereda* administration bureau, the ethnic composition in this *kebele* and the *gots* is heterogeneous. For instance, the Amhara, the Gumuz, the Sinasha, the Agaw and the Oromo live in Menbereselam *got*. In the case of Angtok *got* there are three ethnic groups: the Sinasha, the Oromo and the Gumuz. In the case of the third *got* and focal point of this study, Moga got, the majority (95%) are Gumuz while the rest 5% are the Amhara who settled in the area coming from Wallo eight years ago. Two of the villages in Moga *got* known *Lay Moga* and Dabasa villages were the main sites. These villages are located at twelve and fifteen kms to the east of Dibatie town, the capital of the *wereda*. At these villages the Gumuz reside in significant numbers.

PEOPLE AND LANGUAGE

The Gumuz, Bertha, Sinasha, Mao and Komo are among those groups organized into Benishangul Gumuz region. Other ethnic groups like the Oromo, the Amhara, the Tigre and the Agaw also reside in the region. The major ethnic groups residing in Metekel zone are: the Gumuz, the Sinasha, the Oromo, the Agaw, and the Amhara. Tadesse (1988) also adds that other ethnic minorities like the Kufal, Gonga and Qimant live in Metekel. It is a zone comprising different ethnic groups that speak different languages, socioeconomic structures and cultures.

The Gumuz are said to be the natives with the largest population in the zone (Desalagn, 1988; Waldeselassie, 2002; and Berihun, 1996). According to the report of CSA (1996), the Gumuz comprised 107,495 people, which is 23.3% out of the total 460,459 population of the region. The latest census of the 2007 preliminary census result however describes the number of the population of the region being 670,847. According to the same information the Gumuz are the ones with third highest population figure with a total of 21.11% of the total population next to the Berta 25.9% and the Amhara 21.25% of the total population o the region. In the same source it is reported that, of the total population of the zone estimated to be 201,521, 101, and 134 of them were male, while the rest 100,387 were female. With regard to the number of population on the basis of ethnic groups residing in the zone, the Gumuz consisted 66,965 the next highest ethnic group being the Amhara with a total population of 47,900, Shinansha 32, 037, the Oromo 27,050 Agaw 17,155; the Kambata 2,875; the Hadiya 2,179; and 725 Tigre.

Similar to the case of the regional state and the zone, the largest ethnic group in Dibatie *wereda* is Gumuz accounting for 31% of the population followed by the Amhara and the Oromo, which account 26% and 24% of the population, respectively (CPAR, 2000: 15). The Gumuz in this *wereda* are considered as the indigenous people with the largest number of population.

People at Metekel zone speak languages from the four-language family. The Gumuz speak a language from Nilo Saharan family, the Agaw and the Oromo speak Cushitic language, the Sinasha speak Omotic, while the Amhara are speakers of Semitic language group.

HISTORICAL BACKGROUND

Different scholars have discussed in detail the origin of the Gumuz, the raids and expeditions conducted against the Gumuz by Ethiopian and foreign governments, and the migration of the Gumuz because of these expeditions and taking refugee in their current settlement places and in different parts of the country.

Historical accounts (Ceruli, 1956; James, 1977; 1986; and Tadesse, 1988) record that the Sudanese (Mahadists) and Ethiopian rulers at different times have attempted to control the Gumuz, and describe the exposure of the Gumuz to sporadic slave raid by the highlanders. The raid by the highland rulers is said to be in the 16th and in the main in the17^{th} centuries. According to Tadesse (1988) successive rulers of Gonder, Sarsa Dengil (1563-1597), Susenyos (1607-1632), Fasiladus (1632-1667), Yohannes (1667-1683), and Iyasu the Great (1683-1706), have conducted series of campaigns against the Gumuz. These expeditions have resulted in the imposition of rulers from the neighboring people, the Agaw, over the Gumuz.

Other than the sporadic raids they faced from internal forces, the external forces of the Mahadists have similarly led an expedition against the Gumuz to the south of Abay. James writes that "Conditions were bad at this time in the Blue Nile Valley for the Gumuz people, many of whom fled upstream as far as the Didhessa River as a result of raiding from the Sudan" (1979: 38). James (1986) further reported that they faced the pressure from the Turk-Egyptian government of Sudan, which was conducting slave raid. Scholars who recorded the pressure from internal and external forces say that the Gumuz had to look for ways of escaping the raid by the highlanders and the Mahadists. The raids were said to be a factor for their settlement in lowland areas in order to resist control in the future (James, 1976).

The participation of the Oromo in these expeditions and raids of the Gumuz is also a recorded phenomenon according to historical accounts. Alessandro Triulizi (1986: 52-54) and James (1986: 129-130) have recorded that the rulers of Leqa Naqamte had participated in such raids. Similarly the autobiographical narrative of the son of Kumsa Moreda of Leqa Naqamte (*Dajjazmatch* Yemane Kumsa) similarly witness the fact that these rulers of Wallega used to conduct slave raids among the Gumuz in Didhessa valley, near Mendi, Nadjo, and Gimbi areas, (Meron, 2003). Those people brought from Didhessa valley used to serve in different capacities at the palace of *Dajjazmatch* Kumsa as cooks, guards and entertainers, (Ibid).

With regard to the origin of the Gumuz society there have been different accounts forwarded. Wallmark (1981) writes that the history of the movement of the Gumuz in the 19th century has its origin from parts of Gojjam (Guba and Wambera) then to the south to Wallega as a retreat from taxation, slave raid and serfdom. James (1986) states that the Gumuz of the current Kamashi zone (according to her those to the south of the Abay River) claim to have originated from Gojjam. And she further says that the settlement to the area is a result of the Abyssinian taxation and servitude. The Italian historian Ceruli (1956.15) writes that the origin of the Gumuz used to be the current Awi zone of Amhara Regional State, [Agaw midir in his words].

> According to traditions of the Awiya Agaw, collected by Beke in Agaumidir, the first inhabitants were the Shankala, perhaps the Gunza, who were driven out by the Agaw when they came from Lasta. The Gumuz also had a trouble with the Sidama people called Gonga and Shinansha to the south of their territory, and it is recorded that in the area of Dura River the Shinansha compelled the Gumuz to pay tribute in cereals, meat and honey, under threat of causing drought or excessive rain.

The Gumuz are spread from Metema in the north, south to Metekel (Gojjam) and further south to the Didhessa Valley crossing the Abay River in the south. Similarly my elder informant from *Dabasa* clan, Aiwa Beke, explained such clan names like *"Idangliya"* are indicative of the fact that the Gumuz were once residents in Dangila area in Gojjam. Waldeselassie (2002: 66) similarly documents the account of his informants at Mandura and Dangur which highlights similar story that the Gumuz had once lived in the highlands occupying territory to the east of Zage at Lake Tana and

Bahir Dar in the northeast to south and southwest wards in Dangila, Enjibara, Koso-ber, Bure, Debre Markos up to the Abay River basin bordering Gojjam, Shewa and Wallega to the south and southeast. Thus the stories from informants in both cases suggest that they had once been in Gojjam. The political instability between 1880-1920 in southern Gojjam and consequent wars, raids and disturbances during this time called for the incursion of the Gumuz from Guba into Metekel region and Didhessa Valley (James 1977, 1986: Abdusamad 1989).

Abeyya (2001: 19) traces the migration of the Gumuz to their place of current settlements in Metekel and Didhessa valley to originate from the Sudan: Anguar- Roseires- Dender River- Ethiopian highlands of Gonder and Gojjam -Upper and Lower courses of Abay- Ethiopian Lowlands (Metekel and Didhessa). The Internal factor Abeyya (2001) identified for the migration of the Gumuz is the inter-clan conflict between the Gumuz in Guba in the late 19th Century. He describes the conflict between *Dukunzilla* and *Bugua* clans that resulted in the retreat and defeat of the first one, who traveled to Wallega.

Besides these historical accounts, Waldeselassie (2002) recounts oral tradition about the origin of the Gumuz, which is also a common legend I obtained from informants at *lay* Moga who claim their descent to a common ancestor they call the *key* (non-Gumuz people). Here it is worth quoting Waldeselassie's writing, as it is a common oral tradition told by most Gumuz elders in the two study villages as well.

> Once upon a time twin sons were born from a mother. One of the sons was darker black (Gumuz) and the other was fair-colored (non-Gumuz highlander). As they grew up matured, they contested for power in the presence of the local assembly. First, they were given a horse for galloping where the Gumuz fell down while the latter galloped well. Then, they were offered to choose from bow and arrow on the one hand and spear and shield on the other, the Gumuz taking the former and the non-Gumuz the latter. Again, they were made to choose from *inga* (porridge) and *injera* (pancake like unleavened bread), with the Gumuz favoring porridge while the non-Gumuz favored *injera*. Later, they were asked to settle either to the "right" (in the central highlands) or to the "left" side (towards the periphery). The non-Gumuz chose to settle to the right in the central highlands and the Gumuz chose to settle to the left towards the lowlands and the periphery (Waldeselassie, 2002: 61-64).

The historical documents give a detailed account of the origin of the Gumuz, the sporadic raids by the highlanders and the retreat of the Gumuz to their current locations as mentioned above. Besides, Gumuz informants also emphasize the fact that they are settled at their current settlement patterns after they faced sporadic raids by the highlanders.

SOCIAL ORGANIZATION

The Gumuz are patrilineal society with a segmentary social organization pattern. Most of the families in the study area are nuclear one, where a husband and wife live with their children except a few cases where they are staying with elders (grand parents of the husband). Neighborhood in most cases is formed with members of the same kin group. Sisay (1988) elaborates this point in that the family forming the most important social organization of the Gumuz community. The homestead among the Gumuz is called *demetsa*. People who live in the same hamlet call each other *Soka* (kin). Those kin members residing in the same village form commune. Different territories are assigned to members of different clans. A person thus can clear and use land in the clan's territory if it is unused land. Thus, people related by blood live in a neighborhood and distance in the area of settlements is an indicator of distance in blood relation.

There is a strong relationship between neighbors or members of the commune. This strong relationship is manifested in labor exchange during production activities. In most instances neighbors perform most of the agricultural activities together. Besides, as mentioned earlier the Gumuz use shifting cultivation method in which they leave the land fallow in cases of infertility of the land and they move to other places in search of fertile land. In such movements if the newly allocated farmlands are found to be at some distance from their villages, members of the same commune tend to move their settlement sites close to the new farmland. This in addition to the labor exchange is another fact that explains the close relation between members of the commune.

People from the same clan reside in close villages (in the clan territory). Waldeselassie (2002: 70) states that, "Members of closer kin groups live in villages inside the clan territory". A clan consists of a number of neighborhood kin groups who belong to the same descent in the patrilineal line.

Bender mentions that the Gumuz are divided on clan basis: "The Gumuz have over 100 clans, each named after a tree which the clan founders sat under at the time of the dispersal of the Gumuz people long ago" (Bender, 1975: 61). Berihun (2004) mentions the responsibilities and obligations of members of clan in addition to exogamous marriage being:

> ... Accepting a clan member to settle in a place of his/ her choice and providing support (such as farmland and reciprocal labour when necessary), security (protecting the clan member from being attacked by other clans), sharing ritual offices (*kegidiya*), and the possibility of obtaining (borrowing) a female clan member that a person can exchange for wife (Berihun, 2004: 81).

Desalagn states that clan is further divided into a commune. According to Desalagn (1988: 124) a commune is "a group of families ranging from 20-50 who reside in the same vicinity and who exchange labor in the process of production". Tadesse, (1988: 9) similarly explains such a division among a Gumuz society residing in small-scattered villages "consisting of a few huts belonging to very closely related families with the whole Gumuz area apparently divided into a number of clan territories". Unlike clan commune is constantly in flux: it emerges, grows and disappears depending on the needs of individual members and the demands of the shifting agricultural system" (Desalagn, 1988: 124).

Different factors account for the change in settlement pattern of a given commune among the Gumuz. Due to political factors such as interethnic or intraethnic conflicts they tend to change their places of settlement. Another factor can be economic whereby in a way people tend to move to a new location looking for more productive farms located some distance from the earlier one. Besides, social pressure like over population in a given area might call for further subdivision of communes and occupation of another settlement site. Desalagn (1988) also mentions another cause that due to the order by spirit medium person *gafia* and due to magico-religious factor members of a commune change their settlement.

Members of the same clan distributed over different places are referred in a common territorial group, which is a broader category than the clan. Waldeselassie (2002: 70) discuss the situation in the research zone as "in addition, a number of clans of respective territory form larger broader territorial groups such as the Gumuz of Mandura, Dangur, Gublak, Guba, Dibatie, Wambera, etc".

Berihun (1996) pushes this territorial category further and he explains that a Gumuz individual belonging to territorial groups being separated either by religion or natural barriers like the Muslim Gumuz of Guba, Wambera or as the Gumuz of Mandura, Mambuk etc. Berihun (2004: 85) states that "A territorial grouping is more inclusive than the clan and sub clan division. So the reference in territory of the clans is either taking the location as a ground or religious basis. This territorial division grows further in scale up to a broader territorial reference as to the Gumuz of Metekel, of Kamashi, etc (Waldeselassie, 2002).These different territorial references to the Gumuz add up to form the Gumuz ethnic group (Ibid). Berihun (2004) in his doctorial dissertation mentions that the clan relations is strong and is important at the village level than at the territorial one.

In the social life of the Gumuz the role of elders (*ganzas)* is very important. Community elders play a significant role in the daily lives of the community. They are involved in different family and community affairs. They play an important role in marriage in organizing the different forms of marriage: exchange marriage, marriage by bride wealth payment, abduction, and levirate marriage. Their activities extend from arranging marriages and blessing the couples to solving conflicts arising between married couples and at times of divorce. *Ganzas* are the ones playing a significant role in conflict resolution. They handle conflicts of different levels as the inter clan conflict and intra clan ones. Waldeselassie (2002) explains further that they care for young and weak, they condemn acts such as theft, adultery and crime. In Gumuz community, the contribution of elders in sharing their experiences in the task of production is also significant.

Their contribution in this aspect ranges from selection of fields for production, informing the community the benefit of working in groups, and advising them on how to effectively use resources and ways of conserving them, etc. Many informants suggested that elders are living heritages who pass traditions and histories of the society to the generations and who mould the youngsters' daily activities and lives and who play important role in way of bringing up a new generation aware of his/her histories and traditions.

THE ECONOMIC SCENE

The Gumuz base their living mainly on integral shifting cultivation. James (1976: 86) and Wallmark (1981) have described an integral shifting cultivation being a common practice among the Gumuz to the south of Abbay River. Similarly Abeyya (2002) states that the Gumuz of Kamashi *wereda* practice integral shifting cultivation. Desalagn (1988); Tadesse (1988); Berihun (1996) and Waldeselassie (2002) also highlight the fact that this is a common practice among the Gumuz of Metekel zone.

There are different successive stages in the task of shifting cultivation. The first task is that of site selection. Informants explain that this is the stage that requires due care and they perform it carefully. They also said that the advice from elders and sometimes from *gafias* (magico priests), and ones have prior experiences help in this stage. Such factors as the existence of dense vegetation on the land, its location along valley bottom and slopes are said to be indicators of the fertility of a given land. One has to cut and leave a tree to mark that the land has already been occupied.

After identifying the site the next step is that of clearing it (*kancha*). The trees are cut shorter and the grasses and shrubs are also cleared.

They leave part of the cleared trees, shrubs and grasses on the land for some time until they get dry and then the next stage of burning follows. They leave some trees shorter as they are going to use them as a support to the tree climbing crops to be intercropped. The grasses, shrubs and tress cut down will be left on the field to be dried. The next step is that of burning the cut down trees (*Ufmanja*). With regard to burning there are different reasons as to why they burn. James (1977) and Abeyya (2002) associate it as to make future task of cropping easier. Abeyya further claims that it is done to kill insects and poisonous animals, to make further activities easier, and for hunting. However informants at *Lay* Moga and Dabasa villages consider the activities mentioned above being of secondary importance and the prior purpose according to them is to add to the fertility of the land by using the ashes.

The next stage is that of cropping. At this stage they use simple hand tools to dig holes. They put more than one seed in a hole, as the probability of growing is low. The cropping is arranged in such a way that in most cases they intercrop different crops so as to yield a number of crops in one harvest season. Different crops like tree climbing legumes and root crops are usually cropped with the major cereals. The Gumuz in the study site use one field only two times. They usually crop finger millet in the first round and sorghum in the second. In some cases a person owns more than one field and he uses to crop different cereals on these different fields, say millet and sorghum. After the harvest they leave the land fallow for further regeneration. The land left fallow is called *bakala*. The fallowing period according to informants is three years on average.

The process of leaving a land fallow and the duration of its regeneration takes between ten to fifteen years on average (Desalagn 1988; Abeyya 2002). But my informants emphasize that the fallow period used to be longer in earlier days due to lower number of population and availability of land on a larger scale. They clear another land than using it for growing another crop for the coming cropping season. The man who first cultivated a land and left it fallow is considered as the right owner of it. Leaving earlier farms fallow they have to move to new farmlands. Informants explained that as their commune members occupied most of the land in the vicinity, they are being forced to have their farms at distant places. This sometimes leads to movement of the whole groups as already mentioned above.

The major crops grown in the study area (Moga *got*) are finger millet, sorghum, maize, yam, sesame, hot peeper, pumpkin, and Niger seed. Of these the major food crops produced by the Gumuz mainly for consumption are finger millet, sorghum, maize and pumpkin. Niger seed and sesame are produced mainly for market. According to the Situational Analysis Report of CPAR (2000), finger millet takes the highest share in production of the crops in Dibatie *wareda*, 22% followed by sorghum 21% and maize 18% of the total crop production. The Gumuz in the study sites, produce in most cases for household consumption and they concentrate on the production of grains than the oil seeds.

SUPPLEMENTARY LIVELIHOOD ACTIVITIES

Supplementary to the shifting cultivation there are other means of livelihood activities adopted by the Gumuz community at the study area. Desalagn (1988: 123) points out that, "Hunting and gathering and at times fishing are supplementary endeavors designed to support the shifting cultivation". Hunting and gathering have been described as supplementary liveli-

Names of Gumuz Months and Ethiopian and Gregorian Equivalent

No	Gumuz Months	Ethiopian Equivalent	Gregorian Equivalent
1	*Michzgidibija*	*Meskerem*	September
2	*Iibija*	*Tikimit*	October
3	*Banduha*	*Hidar*	November
4	*Biba*	*Tahisas*	December
5	*Ebagunda*	*Tir*	January
6	*Ebitkaagicha*	*Yakatit*	February
7	*Doka*	*Magabit*	March
8	*Dufazika*	*Mayziaya*	April
9	*Duguchaka*	*Ginbot*	May
10	*Kuanda*	*Sene*	June
11	*Meta*	*Hamle*	July
12	*Dhibija*	*Nahase*	August

hood activities for the Gumuz at different areas. James (1976) also mentions that gathering wild vegetables and fruits as well as hunting different animals is part of the daily diet of the Gumuz society to the south of Abbay. Abeyya (2001) also describes this as a common livelihood strategy among the Gumuz at Kamashi zone (Didhessa Valley). The vegetables collected include root crops, leaves and different wild fruits. The animals hunted for food range from small animals like birds to big games like warthog *(kerkero).*

Other activities like fishing and honey collection are used by the Gumuz at the study area as supplementary means of livelihood. They also use other mechanisms as ways of subsidizing income as brewing local drinks on a small scale, selling firewood and handicraft products, and herding livestock.

BELIEF SYSTEM

The majority of the Gumuz at the study villages of *lay* Moga and Dabasa villages are followers of traditional belief system as in the case of the majority of Gumuz community as a whole. The belief in *Missa* (poly spirit) is an extant tradition among the Gumuz at the study site. Wallmark (1981) says that the Gumuz at Didhessa valley refer to their traditional deity as *Rebba*. Ceruli (1956) also identifies the term *Rebba* that he says has equivalent meaning to *Musa*, which he assumes originating from the Arabic terms Rebbi and Mosses.

The Gumuz allocate different spirits to different activities, events and natural resource, etc. For instance, the sky spirit is referred to as *miss-gokuna*, *miss-aya* is river spirit, *miss-silla* is spirit for hunting, *miss-teha* is delivery spirit, *miss-dema* is rain spirit, etc. *Yamba* is the creator of all living creatures and it is above all *missas* (spirits) and it is *Yamba* that controls the overall function of the *missas* and all living creatures.

There are different spirit mediums that play an important role in the belief system of the Gumuz. There are three of such spirit mediums: *etimass-gideya, gafia, and gola*. The responsibility of these spirit mediums varies. For instance, the first is responsible to inform the community of the annual ritual of *miss-gideya* (*gideya* spirit). This is held once in a year. According to informants in Moga *missjediyas* unlike the other two spirit mediums they are few in number. There is only one *missjediya* in Moga *got* which is a very wide and scattered settlement area. The ceremony is made once in a year following the date set by the spirit medium person and all people prepare *kiya* (local brew) and chicken as a sacrifice to *Missa*. At this event they praise the spirit for the harvest they had and they say a prayer for the coming harvest season, the health of the community. Informants explained that his power is limited to the above event, and that it is a thanksgiving ritual where they ask different *missas* for help.

The second category is *gafia*. According to Waldeselassie, the *gafia* is "a very crucial magico-religious and traditional medicine person who plays a multiple role as a medium between the poly- spirits and the community" (2002: 78). Informants explain that the role of the *gafia* is broader than the first one. Such activities like praying for rain and calamity and asking the spirit of rain is a task of a *gafia*. However, the task of holding the ritual mentioned above is assigned to the *etimassgideya* only. The Gumuz in most cases consult a *gafia* about issues in their daily lives. After spending two days with one of the key informants conducting an in-depth interview, on the third day of the visit, the woman had to consult the *gafia* in the neighborhood about the conversation we had. *Gafias* are also consulted during the time of sickness and they give traditional herbal medicines to the sick person.

Unlike the *etimassgideya* there can be one and more *gafias* in a village and the case of the villages under study is a good manifestation to this fact. Though located at a walking distance from each other there are three *gafias* in the two study villages based on the information I obtained. They are further consulted on issues such as selecting a perfect site and date for hunting and cultivation. *Gafias* in most cases are called to people's places especially in cases of sickness.

The *gola* is a witch doctor that is believed to have more power than the first two. He is believed to be closer to different spirits (*missas*) and to the *Yamba*. The *gola* is believed to have the power to identify complicated cases like causes of a death of a person, theft, crimes, crop destruction, etc. They are believed to have the power of identifying the reasons of the presence of an individual at his place. *Golas* are relatively small in number in a given society.

CHAPTER 4

RITES OF PASSAGE

BIRTH/IMPIQWA AND PREGNANCY FOOD TABOO

The Gumuz attach much value to *impiqwa* (birth). Men consider it as something related to their own privilege and gaining social prestige. There is a common belief that having children is a lifetime process, which needs to keep on going as long as a person is fertile. There is a famous saying in Gumuz language, which explains the importance of having as large number of children as possible: *indapiqu chinka indi guta*, literally meaning giving birth to a large number of children is a blessing.

Women continue their daily routines until the last minute to delivery. The food taboo for pregnant women is one thing which changes during the time of pregnancy. They are educated about these cultural codes related to food taboo at an early age. Rogers (1980: 14) raises change in routine during pregnancy as a common process in some societies "where many western societies see rest as appropriate for women in pregnancy, others hard work and exercise".

During their pregnancy Gumuz women refrain from eating foods which are rich in protein like goat meat, egg, and chicken. Bonvillan (1996) mentions that, in many cultures throughout the world various taboos on specific foods are commonly imposed on women during pregnancy and lactation. She further says that the taboos attached to food for women have religious explanation. Bonvillan (1996: 209) explains this fact as "in some societies cultural norms define gender specific routines for eating and for foods to be eaten".

The taboo related to chicken is abstaining from eating those reared at home although they are tolerable to eat chicken bought from market or exchanged from a neighborhood. They also refrain themselves from eating food cooked by using their in-law's cooking utensils. They do not eat food under preparation and they have to eat after their husbands have first tasted the food (as long as he is alive, even in the absence or death of a husband, the eldest son or the man who has inherited the widow has to taste it first).

Bonvillan (1996) is of the opinion that taboos associated with some societies are result of gender-based division of labour, where women who do not participate in hunting and herding are not allowed to eat meat. The other possible explanation she gives is the gender asymmetries in authority and social status, which she says, can be a result of sexual ranking. The Gumuz on the other hand give a religious explanation for the existent gender disaggregated food taboos. They believe that transgressing the rules lead to punishment by evil spirit and call for anger of *Missa* and a curse. When pregnant women break the rules, it is believed to result in severe labor, maternal death, miscarriage sterility, deformation or sickness of children.

Gumuz women deliver away from their home in bushes, near rivers or at different pinches. Giving birth near granaries and agricultural fields is a taboo. The Gumuz consider bearing the pain of delivery as an indication of being courageous and strong mother. The task of removing the placenta and burying it, cutting the umbilical cord and washing the newborn child are all the responsibilities of the delivering mother. Making too much noise during delivery and the labor is another act that is believed to call for anger of *Missa* .There will be no birth attendant with a delivering woman. A neighbor, a co-wife or a relative of the delivering woman accompany her if she is giving birth to her first child. In such instances the accompanying lady will help and show her the process. Besides the religious explanation attached to bush delivery mentioned above, informants at *Lay* Moga village have some more point that children born in bushes tend to be brave (especially if it is a baby boy he will be a hunter and a successful warrior in the future than those born under trees, or near a river).

After her delivery and having cleaned herself and her child, the woman will return to her home. On her arrival, her husband will slaughter a chicken and put the blood on the forehead of the child and the mother. This is done as a sacrifice to *Missa* for the safe delivery. Skin from the slaughtered chicken is put under the right arm of the newborn child to keep away any sickness or deformations away from the newborn. The average days range between weeks to ten days. During these days women from the neighborhood help her in the household activities. In case of polygamous marriage, co wives are responsible to provide care to the woman, her husband and members of the family.

A lactating woman in the early days after delivery eats warm food. The villagers come to visit her and a person entering the room has to greet her with the words *"Na Mara Missa"* , which literally means, ‚let *Missa* send you his mercy'! An elderly lady living in the village will give her blessing to the new born child and the mother saying;

> *"Nagimha nach Missa gawana*
> Let this gift of *MIssa* stay alive
> *Michigan atomdinag dat dofalwaza".*
> Let it grow in peace".

A woman who has recently given birth usually uses *chicha* (a home made sanitary pad). A woman who has given birth to a baby is considered as unclean and "filthy". Husbands stay (sleep) in separate hut for about a month or two, and during this time they refrain from eating food cooked and served by their wives. In the case of Polygamous family a husband spends most of his time with the other wife or else he builds a *Jibita* (a small hut which is constructed close to the main house). Moreover, the mother is served in different *faga* (drinking cup) and plate, which will be thrown away after she starts carrying on her daily activities. Informants have explained that in earlier times women who gave birth used to stay outside the house for about two weeks. They mentioned that they used to stay in a separate hut (*jibita*) as they were considered as unclean.

CHILD SEX PREFERENCES AND TRADITIONS OF NAMING CHILDREN

As it is the case in most parts of Ethiopia, the Gumuz value male off springs higher. They consider the birth of a baby boy as having a person who could take over the responsibility in the family in the absence or death of the father, and who could also inherit the father's property. The value attached to a female baby is essentially in labour provision and benefit from exchanging them in marriage. Giving birth to a baby girl is a blessing for the purpose of their socioeconomic values in the society. According to informants Gumuz mothers especially take it as an opportunity of getting someone who will be sharing the burden of hard work. Men also welcome the birth of a female baby who can be exchanged for marriage and for other social purposes, to be discussed under the following chapters.

The right of naming a child is exclusively that of husbands/ fathers. The reason given for this is that it is the men who are in charge of managing every family matter. The tradition of naming a newborn baby among the Gumuz has different aspects. The first case is where children are named after different individuals. In this case they name children after the name of a guest who arrived at the village either on the eve of the delivery or right after it. The other way of naming is related to the tradition of naming after the place of delivery. As mentioned above delivery usually takes outside of a house, those children born under a tree called *faqa* are called *Wafaqa* and girls born at the same place would be called *Yofaqa.* The other way of giving name to a child is on the bases of the day it was born. If a person is born on Wednesdays, Saturdays (market days in the area); he will be referred to as *Wagab*e while girls born on these days will be called Y*agabe*, which is derived from a Gumuz term *gaba*, market. Children are also named after months, when they were born.

The Gumuz name their children after different political regimes and political developments at regional and national levels. For instance, in one Gumuz family in the study area, there was a case where the father is called *Dergu* (referring to the socialist military regime in Ethiopia 1974-91*)* while his two children born after the time of Ethio-Eritrea border conflict are named after the two conflicting parties as *Shabiya* and *Wayane* (Referring to the Eritrean Libration Front and the Tigrean Libration Front). They do not name their children after the name of a thief, a person having mental problem and an evil eye.

Although girls are beneficial to the society, they are always considered as someone who will be abandoning the village on marriage. Nevertheless, the Gumuz welcome the birth of baby girls, they always prefer the first-born baby to be a boy. The first-born boy will have the privilege of using his younger sisters in exchange at the time he is ready for marriage. If the first child is a girl, her relatives will be the ones benefiting by exchanging her than her own brother, who will otherwise be offered the chance first. Although having a girl is valued as being associated with her future productive, reproductive roles and her exchange value, boys are valued more and the Gumuz prefer to have the first-born baby boy due to the social prestige to be obtained by having a son.

CHILDREN BORN OUT OF WEDLOCK

In the study area, there are cases where children are born out of wedlock the most common factor for this being rape. In those cases where a man rapes a virgin girl and impregnates her, he will be forced to marry her. Besides, he is expected to give another girl in exchange to the victims' clansmen.

The other case is when a man sleeps with a married woman and impregnates her. The Gumuz consider this as a more offensive case. In most cases such an act invites conflict. In this case the person will be forced by elders to pay compensation, in most cases three goats and two hundred *birr*. The goats paid in compensation will be slain and the meat will be served to the elders. The blood of the animal is considered as symbolizing the control of bloodshed, which would have been caused as a result of revenge. The couples (the raped wife and her husband) do not eat the meat as it is considered impure. The child born of this encounter, if any, will be named after the name of the woman's husband (not his biological father). Her husband will have every right over the child.

During the field work in February 2005, I happened to attend one case, which the elders at *lay* Moga village were dealing with. In that incident, Yoke Admasu a young girl from *Dibishwua* clan, who was married to a man from *Dabasa* clan had a disagreement with her husband and moved to her father's place. During her stay in her father's place a man from *Dibisariya* clan raped her and she became pregnant. The case was handled in such a way that the man was forced to pay two heads of cattle and a goat as a compensation for his misdeed. One of the elders handling the case mentioned that, as Yoke's case and her husband's disagreement was not yet settled, if their relationship ends in divorce, the man would be forced to marry her. And if the case with her husband is solved with Yoke going back to her husband, the child would be named after her husband and he will have the right that a biological father has over his daughters.

SOCIALIZATION OF CHILDREN

Children among the Gumuz are taught about their roles at early age. This is also said to be a common way of socializing children in most parts of the country. With regard to such pattern of early role identification, Andromeda (1968: 30) says that "following the delivery of a child custom and the announcement of sex and the course of his life there after, boys are taught to be courageous, domineering and to show qualities of leadership, while girls are taught to be submissive, conservative, self spoken and shy".

Similarly the socialization in Gumuz society is done in such a way that, young boys are advised to be courageous, and outspoken. The division of labour on the basis of gender starts at early age. Young girls learn at their early age some household chores. Mothers are responsible for socializing their daughters. Around the age of five they start cleaning the house and carrying for siblings. At this early age they will be busy looking after their siblings, caring and feeding them in the absence of the mothers.

Around the age of seven, they will be sent to fetch water. Besides, as of this age they are believed to be matured enough to go to bushes with their friends and carry some firewood for the household consumption. Mothers will train their young girls on how to grind grains and cook *Inga* (porridge) at this age. As of the age of nine to ten a Gumuz girl is believed to be ready to perform all the domestic activities on her own while her mother is busy with the farm activity. It is common among the Gumuz for a young girl to carry out her jobs with a young siblings on her back. Besides doing such household activities, a Gumuz girl will be trained on how to be an ideal wife in the future. Such information as the need to wash their future husband's leg on his return from long travel and having a long day as well as kneeling down while serving pond water in presence of his clan members are some of the norms they will be informed at this early age. Their mothers share with them about the gender-disaggregated pregnancy food taboos, the taboos attached to menstruation and lactation.

Young girls unlike their age mate young boys are expected to spend longer hours at home. On the other hand, the first activity assigned to young boys at an early age is the training he receives on how to hunt small animals especially birds while herding cattle. This is usually done by the time he reaches the age of six to eight (before circumcision). An arrow and bow is the first gift of a father to his son. In case of conflict, he would be warned to defend himself. The common task assigned to a child boy is herding cattle, where he is expected to hunt birds to eat and which will give him the chance of spending time out of home. At their teen ages both boys and girls keep on performing the above activities along which they will be involved in activities on farm.

Table 3 – Gender based Division of Labour at Early Ages

Age	Roles of girls	Roles of boys
5-7	– Cleaning house, caring for siblings	– Playing with their age mates
7-10	– Fetching water, collecting wood and grinding grain, cooking	– Time to learn hunting and herding cattle
Teenagers	– Performing the above activities and helping on farm of parents.	– Mainly concentrating on the new role i.e. help on farm work and participating in different labour organizations. – At the age of fifteen and above he will be having his own plot of land which he will be farming and saving the money he obtained by selling the products

Source: Compiled from field Notes

Though the overall literacy rate of the society is low, girls are the ones with the least access to education. The explanation given by informants to why girls are denied such rights basically refer to three general factors. The first factor is that, there is a strong feeling among Gumuz parents that, as girls are going to be given in marriage to another clan, it is unworthy to invest in their education. The second reason given by most informants is that girls who have been allowed to spend time out of their home and far from their villages will end up disobeying their parents and they will not have time to learn the domestic chores, which are believed to be valued more in their future lives. The third factor is related to the insecurity of their travel to and back from school due to the threat of abduction.

The data obtained from the district education bureau (2005) report on number of students is good evidence to the existing gender imbalance in the enrolment rate both at the *wereda* and *kebele* level.

Table 4 – Student Enrollment Rate at Dibatie Secondary School on the bases of Ethnic group and Gender

Ethnic group	9th		10th		11th		12th	
	M	*F*	*M*	*F*	*M*	*F*	*M*	*F*
Gumuz	11	–	2	–	1	–	–	–
Shinansha	104	41	42	21	15	2	15	1
Oromo	108	40	61	15	16	7	13	2
Amhara	67	42	27	7	5	1	4	1
Agaw	31	25	8	7	5	–	–	–

Source: Dibate wereda Educational Bureau 2005 report

In the *kebele* where this research was conducted, Angtok *kebele*, there is only one elementary school, the Angtok Elementary School where the total number of male students from grade 1-4 (first cycle) is two hundred and thirteen while that of girls is only ninety-eight. There is no second cycle (grades 5-8) at the *kebele* and students go to the *wereda* town for that.

RITES OF PASSAGE

GUMUZ GIRLS INITIATION

The first menstruation is considered as an event marking a rite of passage and a transition of a girl to the stage of womanhood. It is a stage, which the Gumuz believe marks that a girl is matured enough for marriage, to have a child and take responsibility.

On the onset of first menstruation a girl informs her closest friend as it is a taboo to talk about it in public. It is the girl's friend that will be informing her friend's mother to prepare the ritual of blessing. A small hut (*Jibita*) will be built outside the main house. This is because if girls stay in the main house and happened to drop menstrual blood such an act is believed to call for anger of house spirit (*musa- misa*). The girl's friend and the menstruating girl will stay in the hut during the first menstruation. The girl will be fed by her accompanying friends because eating by her own hands as her body during this first cycle of menstruation is believed to be poisoned and highly unclean. During these days she hardly talks with her friend. Most of the taboos at this stage resemble that of the aftermath of the delivery. The *faga* (wooden cup) she uses for her drinks and the plate are separate ones. In some cases these utensils will be thrown away after the first period. But in most cases she will be using the utensils every month until she leaves for her husband's village and she keeps them in the *Jibita*. Gumuz girls and women prepare traditional sanitary pads called *chicha*, which is produced from a tree called *faqa*. They immerse the leaves of this plant in water for hours and grind it. Asking one's friend for *chicha* is a taboo and a woman has to be ready and have her own.

Anthropologists have underscored the universal importance of menstruation by documenting how the event is interwoven. Buckley (1988) in the *Blood Magic* discusses that there are different taboos associated with menstruation in most societies in the world. Similarly Weideger (1977) in the book *Menstruation and Menopause* mentions that it is a universal phenomenon, which cannot be interpreted without analyzing the culturally situated meaning in different societies. Sandy (1981) identifies five major different types of taboos on the basis of statistical analysis of one hundred and fifty six societies. These are: ban on sexual intercourse; restrictions on activities and contacts with other people; taboos against contacts with men's ritual equipment and weapons; taboos on cooking and handling food, and total seclusion in a separate hut. These five different types of taboos are also some of the taboos attached to menstruation among the Gumuz society as it is stated in the ethnographic material.

The girl's mother informs it to her husband and they prepare a feast before the second menstruation. Unseth as quoted by Waldeselassie (2002: 72) describes this event as "girls are not circumcised; their coming of age is marked by singing. All the villagers will visit her a month later, presenting her with a chicken and singing special songs".

After their first menstruation, the young girls have to refrain themselves from approaching uncircumcised boys and men (even their brothers and fathers). Until the feast of celebrating the first menstruation is held menstruating girls are not allowed to enter the main house, as they are considered unclean. Failure of organizing the feast before the next menstruation is believed to cause misfortune to members of the family. Even in cases where parents do not have the money to be spent on such feasts they borrow money from close relatives and the extent of the feast to be held depends upon the economic status of the parents. In a well to do family the number of goats to be killed can exceed five and they kill oxen. And the *kiya* brewed needs to be enough to serve all who attend the ritual.

On the day of the celebration her close friend will wash her body taking her to a nearby river. An adult woman from the village shaves the girl's hair. They decorate her hair with *gifqa* (a decorative red mud). On her return from the river, her father slaughters a goat and after this ritual of sacrifice the girl is allowed to enter the main house. This event is said to clean the girl. It is following such an occasion that the menstruating girls start talking and having time with members of the family and the villagers.

The initiation ceremony according to local traditions is described as "a mouse opening ceremony" (which marks the time when the taboos set on the girl due to the menstruation come to an end). With the blessing elders spit *kiya* on the body of the girl and she is also made to do so by spiting it on the ground. After this ceremony she is allowed to talk to close relatives and friends of the family who bring food and drinks to be served at the feast. The first menstruation also sets the start of the food taboos as in eating *boy*a (root crop), *kim*a, and pepper which are believed to call for anger of *Missa* and to make them infertile.

Though such a celebration is an occasion happening only once in a lifetime, the menstrual seclusion and food taboos attached to menstruation are things that remain with the woman until menopause. The taboos associated with menstruation include: refraining from touching the household utensils, opening and closing gates of the main house, sitting on stools, washing her body, cooking, brewing *kiya,* passing through farm, getting near grain farms and touching grains, shaking hands and sleeping on beds. The only facilities in *Jibita* are a sleeping ground, a *faga* (cup), a plate and *chichas* to be used. Berihun (2004: 137) mentions some of the menstrual taboos saying,

Women are not allowed to participate in agricultural work during menstruation as they are banned to cross a certain area of the hut or to enter the main house (depending on the regional variations). This is part of the belief in *misa* (super natural being), that women should not be in close contact with sacred places and *misa* during such times.

The case discussed below elaborates this issue:

A Woman at her late thirties from Dibudiya clan came to Yatinkish's (one of the key informants) place while I was interviewing Yatinkish. The woman came to ask Yatinkish to send her daughter to help her with cooking food to the family. The woman did not enter the main house we were in. They were talking about the issue in laud voices. I asked Habte (the interpreter) about what these women were discussing and he explained to me that she was asking for help. While I was leaving for my room, I went to see the woman and I found her at home carrying her son, while the girl she called from Yatinkish's place was doing the cooking. I was surprised to see the woman disobeying one of the taboos attached to menstruation. I spent an hour with the woman and I had a chance of asking her questions related to the issue of menstruation and the taboos attached to it in details. It was at this point that I came to realize about the exception of such cases.

CIRCUMCISION OF BOYS

Circumcision of boys around the age eight to ten is an event that marks their rite of passage to maturity. The Gumuz do not circumcise girls. Circumcision of young boys marks the initiation ceremony for boys. There are skilled persons, who are qualified to perform the circumcision. Circumcision in most cases is done in group and this according to informants is because the boys can encourage each other and they can stay together until their wounds recover. Boys circumcised together in most cases remain lifetime friends who share their gains and pains. There are some taboos for the circumcised boys. The circumcised boys have to stay in a hut, where they will be cleaning the wound using medicines the circumciser gives them. They stay in separate hut but unlike the menstrual seclusion their seclusion is not due to being unclean. The reason for their seclusion is more for safety purpose in that if they make contact with people and if other people happen to see their wounds, it would take longer to get cured. During their time of seclusion and in between the time of the recovery and the feast to be held, these boys will be referred to as *Sampa* meaning" a circumcised person".

Each young circumcised boy will eat on a separate plate and all the utensils he uses are exclusively his. During this period, they have to take care so as not to have eye contact with people who serve them food and drink. When the boys recover from the wound an initiation ceremony will be held. The boys wash each other's body and their hair will be shaved. On such an initiation ceremony food and drinks will be prepared. There will be dancing and singing during the feast. It is only on the onset of such initiation ceremony that boys enter the main house. As in the case of girls, elders give their blessings to the boy to be a hero, successful hunter, and defender of his clan, successful in his production and to have a fertile and mannered wife.

DEATH/MISHA

The extent of mourning for a deceased person among the Gumuz depends upon the age of the person. To start with young children, both for uncircumcised boys and young girls before the first menstruation, the mourning is not taken seriously. Parents of the child can perform the funeral themselves and only relatives in the vicinity and neighbors will be informed about it. The funeral usually takes place soon after the death of a child unlike that of adults.

The death of a teenager and unmarried young boy or girl is a very sad event. This is mainly due to the fact that he/she passed away before having a child, to which the Gumuz give much value. The mourning for a sterile person is similarly serious.

Gumuz women have an essential social role with regard to their contribution on the time of a death of a person in the society. It is the eldest daughter of the deceased person or that of his relative (if he does not have one) who is responsible to wash and cover the body . . .

On the death of an aged person, they use a musical instrument called *tora* (a flute) and they beat a*serma* (drum) to announce the villagers about it and to call them to the funeral. Unlike during the death of babies, relatives living at distance places will be called upon to attend the funeral ceremony. The responsibility of informing those relatives is that of young boys in the village. The bereaved family has to wait for the arrival of the relatives for the burial and they preserve the body using a traditional medicine called *qoshe*. This is a powder that they put on the body. The other medicine called *ishitiwa* is mainly used for the purpose of keeping the room from bad smell. They pour it with water and drop it around the place where the body lies and this also is believed to protect termites from damaging the body. Women in the society are the ones responsible for collecting such medicines and preparing the powder.

Upon the death of an old person, the long life he/she had is considered as something to be celebrated. This is mainly because they have to praise the spirits, which gave him such a long life. On this occasion the hunting prowess and other accomplishments of the deceased will be told in praise songs. *Akosa* is a traditional play usually held during funeral ceremonies of aged persons. Young girls play the *assisa* (a musical instrument put on legs) at the party. Young girls decorate their body while attending such a funeral party. The graveyard the Gumuz use is very close to the house. This is due to the belief that if there is a distance between it and the main house, evil spirits and enemies of the deceased person will take away the corpse. Tree or stone usually marks the burial place.

In most parts of Ethiopia, carrying the body to the grave yards is the duty of men. Women among the Gumuz on the other hand participate in it as it is believed that they are strong enough. If enemies kill a person, it is only the females who take part in all tasks of washing the body, digging the graveyard and burying the dead body. This is because a retaliation is a common practice among the Gumuz and it is believed that if a boy/a man from the deceased persons clan happened to see the dead body he will loss the courage for such a retaliation. As women are always from another clan who come to the area in marriage, and as they are seen as outsiders usually the task of burying a person killed by an enemy is left for them.

Tazkar is a memorial feast for a dead person, which is usually held some time after the burial is over. The time of the feast and its size depends upon the economic standard of the deceased family. *Tazkar* is usually held for elders and the size of the feast also depends on the age of the deceased person. But in most cases *tazkar* is not held for women and young children unless the woman is aged. Even in those cases where a *tazka*r is held for women, informants explained that it is relatively lower in size than that of held for men. People coming to the feast contribute different foods and drinks, and there will be dancing and singing on such a ritual. In some cases the feast might extend to three days if the person has many children who can share the expenses among themselves.

CHAPTER 5

GENDER BASED DIVISION OF LABOR

The first question that comes to mind in discussions related to gender based division of labour is who does what. In order to answer such basic question in the process of understanding the gendered roles, one needs to address the topic thoroughly. Discussing the gender based division of labor in any group can clarify the interdependence and cooperation of women and men in the work relationships and who does what and also to identify if there is the aforementioned correlation between type of agricultural technology and gender role in production in the models suggested by Boserup and Goddy.

Gender roles as it has been mentioned under chapter three are the tasks and activities that a culture assigns to the sexes. They are learned behaviors in a given society setting some activities, tasks and responsibilities as exceptional duties of male or female. Gender roles vary considerably across settings. Moser (1998: 27-28) elaborates the concept of gender-based division of labor as follows. She explains the triple roles of reproductive, productive, and community managing activities as:

> Women's work includes not only reproductive work, the child bearing and rearing responsibilities, required to guarantee the maintainace and reproduction of the labour force. It also includes productive work, often as secondary income earners. In rural areas this usually takes the form of agricultural work. In urban areas women frequently work in informal sector enterprises located either in the house or neighborhood. Also women undertake community-managing work around the provision of items of collective consumption, undertaken in the local community in both urban and rural contexts.

Similar to most societies, among the Gumuz men and women have different roles and responsibilities, which in most cases are socially constructed. Women are responsible for all household chores in addition to the support they provide in agriculture and livestock production. Hanna (1990) and Dejene (1989) argue that in the context of Ethiopia, despite the major roles of women in a society and though they shouldered the household chores, women's function at social, economical, political and administrative level was not considered significant.

In order to bring a clear image of the women and girls among the Gumuz society it is a perquisite to address these roles and contributions they have in different activities. Thus, in this chapter the role of women among the Gumuz society in the triple roles mentioned above will be dealt with details.

PRODUCTIVE ROLES OF WOMEN

The productive role refers to activities of women and men that produce economic resources in cash or in kind. Women's role in agriculture and food security is said to be critical in Sub-Saharan Africa. However numerous studies point out the lack of visibility of their participation, contribution in agriculture and development in general. In most cases there is a generalization that men are the main breadwinners in a family and the ones who are contributing on a larger scale. Bossen (1981: 341) highlights this point as "the use of the "head" concept implicitly diminishes the economic roles of women..." The other concept that underplays the significant economic role of women is their lower case of involvement in the paid labor (Boserup 1970).

Gender based division of labor in productive activities as discussed in the third chapter is quite heterogeneous and responsive to changing means of production. It differs among communities on the basis of type of economic activity under practice. The productive roles of women among the Gumuz society in the study area can be seen from different angles such as from their role in the major subsistence activities and supplementary subsistence activities (subsidiary livelihood activities) as to be discussed under these different categories in details.

GENDER BASED DIVISION OF LABOR IN THE HOE FARMING

Berihun (2004) mentions that, men and women among the Gumuz society actively participate in the agricultural activity. "Agricultural activities among the Gumuz are an occupation of both men and women. Although the division of labor seems to follow gender differences, as it applies to most activities, there is no major gendered differentiation in terms of participation (Berihun, 2004: 135). The division of labor in the hoe based farming on the bases of gender is not strict among the Gumuz. Both participate in different activities and there are also some activities that are considered exclusive roles of male and female in the society.

As it has been discussed under chapter three the basic livelihood activity of the Gumuz society is integral shifting cultivation where most of the agricultural activity is done by using simple hand tools. In order to have a clear image of the existing gender based division of labor in the hoe-based agriculture, it is necessary to address the gender roles in the different stages of this basic livelihood activity.

The first task in the cultivation process is the site selection. As it has been discussed in the third chapters in such cases elders are the major role players. Men are the ones responsible for selecting the farmland. Besides, the role of *gafias* is also significant. The contribution of women at this stage is limited to cases where a female *gafia* happened to be consulted on the matter, which is a very rare case. Thus the major decision makers on the selection of site of the farm are men who make the decision without consulting their wives. The justification given for women's denial of such rights is the existing strong ideology that women do not have knowledge on issues like the productivity of a given land.

The following process *Kancha* (Clearing) in most cases is done in a group of communal labour organization (*keamalaya*). Berihun describes this as " one occasion in which gender differences becomes important is related to clearing of big trees in acquiring new plots (*kanchas*), which is men's work" (Berihun, 2004: 135). In this case the duty of men in a given household is to mobilize the neighborhood people for the activity. The person mobilizing such a communal labour party has to prepare the food and drinks to be served to the participants. The preparation of the drink (*Kiya*) and grinding the grain for making the *inga* (porridge), and preparing the food are all the duties of women. The time required for performing the activities of food and drinks preparation increases as the size of the farm increases.

Much of the task of clearing is performed by a group of men while most of the activities related to food and drink preparation is to be handled by an individual woman at the household. The only help for the woman comes at the time of transporting the drink and the food she prepared to the field when the neighboring women will lend their hands. According to informants, in instances where a given household is unable to mobilize a large labor force and when the size of the farm is small, women and young boys in a household will also participate in the clearing. At the next stage of burning (*Ufmanja*) there are defined roles to both sexes. The role of women precedes the burning. Women on the eve of the burning have to collect some firewood from the site selected for the farming and carry it to the house. This task of carrying the firewood home is exclusively that of women. Male family members burn the shrubs and grasses. Unlike the other stages, this stage does not require a labor organization.

The following stage is that of cropping. This is the stage when two activities are carried out at the same time; hoeing (*malaya*) and cropping (*moshtaqa*). At this stage both men and women participate in different activities. The *keamalaya* (communal labour gathering) of both sexes is mobilized at this stage. The role of women starts at the very beginning when they transport seeds to the farm. This is an exclusive activity to be carried out by women, which is defined by the tradition of the society. The next task of women is that of hoeing. Both men and women have *tabas* (hoes). Men also participate in this task though it is on lower scale to that of women. The major role of men in this process is sowing. Sowing is a task to be exclusively accomplished by men.

The other role of women at this stage is preparing and serving *kiya* to members of the labour force, which as mentioned above requires time and energy. As the farm in most cases is located some distance from their living places, this adds to the burden on women who travel all the way carrying the food and drinks to be served, and who have earlier carried the seed to the farm place and who spend their day in digging. Women's participation in these productive activities requires more of their time and energy as they are in most cases burdened with such multiple activities.

The participation of women in the weeding (*madiltaqa*) according to informants is very significant. The participation of men in this activity is conditional being limited only in those instances when the size of the plot is large one. It is women and children in a family who are believed to be responsible for performing the activity. In such cases women mobilizing a *keamalaya* of women in the neighborhood for whom they will be serving *kiya* (local brew).

In cases where the size of their farm is smaller, they leave the weeding to their wives and children. The participation of men in weeding is always accompanied by the organization of labor festive. Men in a given household participate in the task of weeding on the large plot of land where they organize a labor commune accompanied by festivals. In cases when such labor commune is organized, the role of women extends to the preparation of food and drink to those that help in the weeding.

Both men and women will participate at the stage of harvesting (*imtaqa*). However, the task of piling up the harvested crops is that of women. Prior to the harvest, which is done in groups, the contribution of women includes food preparation and serving to those participating in harvesting.

Unlike the food preparation for the preceding stages, here women usually boil some crops like *boya*, which in most cases are intercropped with the crops to be harvested. As the harvest season is the time when different fruits, and leaves are available on a large scale, this (boiling on the site) is a common pattern among the Gumuz on harvesting day. On a harvest day women carry pots to the farm place in the morning for the purpose of boiling some roots, and leaves to serve them to the labor party. Women gather such crops in the middle of the harvest and boil to serve it with the *kiya*. To sum up the activities of women at this stage include transporting cooking materials to the farm place, carrying the drinks to be served on the occasion, participating in the harvesting and piling up the harvested crops. Pilling up of the harvested crops is an exclusive role for women as any activity related to carrying things, is considered as that of women. Women cover the *danzas* (crop pilled before threshing).

Coming to the last activity in the cultivation process, threshing (which is interchangeably called *chida*, *tibisa*), the major role players are men. Similar to the earlier stages it is done in groups. Though women do not take part in threshing they are the ones responsible from the preparation of the threshing ground. Women are expected to prepare and carry the food and drink to the farm place. At this stage the duty of women extends to the task of storing the grains. This task of carrying the grains in a basket to the granaries, which in most cases are located some distance from the farm place and the living areas, is that of women and young girls in the community. Women carry grains weighing thirty to fifty kilos all the way to the granaries. As the second field trip to this study was in the harvesting season, there was a chance of observing women's contribution in the harvesting and threshing activities. After threshing men mostly go to their villages and drink *kiya,* while women usually are engaged in the task of transporting the grains.

On this occasion women also mobilize a labour force for carrying the grains. Such activities of transporting goods and grains are usually left to women who are believed to have more physical strength. A unique thing about the Gumuz society is the common attitude both sexes have about the strength and capability of women to perform activities that require labor. This shows that the "Strength Theory", which explains that strength accounts to the division of labor between male and female, is invalid in the case of the Gumuz society.

Besides serving food and drinks to the women who participated in carrying the grains, women mobilizing the labor force usually give participants some grain of their harvest. The amount of the grain to be given to the women participating in the activity depends on the amount of the total product and the maximum is two baskets, which weighs about five kilos each. Women use the grain for household consumption and they do not keep the grain they obtained in this way or even mix it with their own products. It has to be kept in some other container until consumption.

The participation of women in some agricultural activities like sowing, threshing and harvesting is believed to result in low yield. The justifications given for this are mainly two. The first is related to the religious explanation that their participation in these activities calls for anger of *Missa.* The other reason is related to the dominant view in the lower capacity of women to perform the mentioned activities and thus their participation will result in law yield.

As the above discussion illustrates, the productive role of women in the hoe-based agricultural activity is a very significant one where they actively engage at the different stages. Such tasks as pilling harvested crops, storing grains, carrying seeds to the farm and preparing and carrying food and drinks to the farm are considered to be exclusive roles of women. The ambiguity in the strength theory can best be seen from the case of the Gumuz women. Those tasks, which require strength, are in all cases reserved for women and young girls in the society. There is a famous saying in Gumuz language, *gafa dida anga alma dawit, Gunza anga achinangu* literally meaning women have more strength than men and they can better perform arduous activities than them. From the discussion above it becomes clear that most of the activities men perform (clearing, sowing, harvesting and threshing) are carried out by mobilizing the labor force while the duties of women like food and drink preparation are in most cases done by an individual woman. The work of women in different seasons is not limited to the work on farm. Besides their enormous contribution they are expected to carry out the daily reproductive activities, which will be covered under the following section.

Summary Table for the Gender based division of labour in hoe agriculture

Activity	Role of women	Role of Men
Site selection	– Participation is limited	– Consulting elders and *gafias* about the suitable farmland – Identifying the plot
Kuancha (Clearing)	– Preparation of food and drinks for the labour festive – Carrying the food and drink to the farm place	– Cutting and clearing trees and grasses with the help of Invited labour and women
Ufmanja (Burning)	– Collecting fuel wood before the burning takes Place. – Preparing food for the family members who participated in the burning. – Carrying fuel wood home	– Burn the trees and shrubs

Activity	Role of women	Role of Men
Hoeing (*Malaya*) Sowing (*Moshtaqa*)	– Transporting the seeds to the farm place – Participating in hoeing – Preparing and transporting food and drink to the labour contribution	– Hoeing – Sowing
Weeding (*Madiltaqa*)	– They are the major role players in weeding with the help of their children – If the size of the land is large and on the organization of a labour force, they prepare food and drinks and carry to the site.	– Participation is conditional and it depends on the size of land
Harvesting (*Imtaqa*)	– Piling the harvested crops – Collecting different leaves and root crops and boiling to serve to those participating in the activity. – Carrying *kiya* to the farm place and serving it – Participating in the harvesting	Perform harvesting
Threshing (*Chida*)	– Preparing the food and drinks to be served and transporting it to the farm	– They play active role in the threshing
Storing grains	– Preparing *kiya* for the women participating in transporting the grains – Carrying the grain to the granaries	

Source: Compiled From Field Notes, February 2005

In terms of intra-household allocation of labor, the literature on gender relations in Sub-Saharan African agriculture indicate that women work longer hours than men because of their triple responsibilities which keeps them busy working on fields as unremunerated family labor and undertaking domestic labor (Bryson, 1995 (Moser, 1998).

Men among the Gumuz society typically play their roles in the agricultural production sequentially focusing on a single productive role. Women on the other hand, play their roles simultaneously, balancing it with their reproductive roles of child- bearing, rearing, and caring for young, old and sick members of the family. Women participants in the focus group discussion explained that, "with such workloads, women often age prematurely as carrying heavy loads over long distances is physically demanding and exhausting work". Men also have a strong feeling that an ideal wife is a one who works hard. The common saying is that *"Itaan gafa gunzuma dafahu"*, which means a hard workingwoman lets her husband to have more leisure time.

GENDER BASED DIVISION OF LABOUR IN THE SUBSIDIARY LIVELIHOOD ACTIVITIES

HUNTING

Besides the purpose of providing food, hunting among the Gumuz has a significance of adding to one's social prestige. It is considered as an exclusive task of men. However, it is women who in most cases initiate their husbands to hunt. Before group of people go for hunting, they rehearse the prayer words:

> *Nachi Missa sila gimigihima etarasa*
> *Nag higara changha*
> *Mat onansu minsima nagha gara gawana*
> *let Missa silla (hunting spirit) make our*
> *trip safe and successful delivering*
> *us from misfortunes and dangers.*

In most cases they put *waga* (traditional medicine) on the *chara* (the sharp edge of an arrow) used for hunting. They believe that medicines have power to ensure a successful hunting. *Waga* is made from the root of plants and there are few experts for making it. Women are not participating in hunting but in some case there are women experts who have the knowledge of making *waga*. Nor they eat animals hunted with an arrow, as they believe that eating such game meat will cause a serious health problem. They only eat animals hunted with a gun.

Women also benefit from the prestige of their husbands gained by hunting big games. After killing some big animals like hyena, lion, and buffalo men will be spending some time in exclusion at *Jibita*. A feast will be held for the honorification of the hunter (*gumza dwa*). The heroic man only sleeps with his wife/wives after this ritual. The indirect Wives/Women's privileges from the prestige of successful hunting is manifested on occasions such as fetching water when the wife is given the priority to fetch, she also receives gifts in cash and kind during the ritual ceremony, and she will be the first to be served in a labour party and other social gatherings.

The ritual to be held for a successful hunter is called *a kemasha*. This ritual is mainly held to clean him from the danger that might other wise arise from the spirit of the game hunted. He will be chanting and bragging in the presence of the people attending the ritual. At such ceremonies hunters and their wives will be having separate seats. The other social prestige to be obtained from such a successful hunting is the right of inheriting his brother's wife on the death of his brother. On the death of his brother he will be the one to be offered the right of inheriting the wife, children if any, and the property of his deceased brother. Elders offer their blessings on such a ritual and this blessing is called *imicha*.

The role of women in hunting apart from the task of initiating their husbands also extends to the preparation of such a hunting ritual party. They prepare the food and drinks to be served on the occasion. Wives also give due respect to successful hunters. Such respects are expressed by washing his leg. Thus the Gumuz hunt for food and also for the purpose of the social prestige to be obtained from a successful hunting.

FISHING

Fishing is another supplementary means of livelihood among the Gumuz. The major source of fishing in the study area is a river called Dura and other small streams. They employ different methods of fishing. The different methods employed shape the involvement of women in the fishing activity. The first one is a method of fishing using medicine or through dazing the fish. The medicine is usually put in the upstream and they catch the fish dazed through this method using *iha* (circular net with a wooden edge). Women and young boys use this method of fishing.

February and March are the months when the Gumuz will be fishing on a large scale. During these dry months the water is clear enabling them to use arrow and bow for fishing, which is the second method they employ. Men exclusively use this second method. Women are not only prohibited from fishing using this method but also they do not eat fish hunted using arrow and bow, as it is believed to cause a serious health problem to women, which can even kill them. In the dry season women go fishing in groups and they use *iha* for fishing, as these months of the year are considered to be safe than the rainy season when the rivers are full. The other method is where they use hooks called *jibada* for fishing. This again is a method exclusively used by men. Informants at *Lay Moga* have a different fishing tradition. This method is used in the rainy seasons. People of the village go to a nearby river where they will be fishing. They take with them *kiya*. They drop the *kiya* in the river and say a prayer and ask for a successful fishing. The fishing is done early in the morning on the next day. Therefore, both sexes among the Gumuz participate in fishing depending on the fishing season and the methods to be employed.

HONEY PRODUCTION

The Gumuz mostly use gathering as supplementary sources of food during the time of food shortage. Gathering is a role played mainly by the Gumuz women. Women gather different roots, leaves and fruits by the time they go to bushes to collect firewood. They use different parts of plants: leaves, roots and fruits for food. Some of the most favorable root crops gathered by the Gumuz women are *echa*, *emakiba*, and *yaaga*. *Patwa* (pumpkin) is another root crop favored by the Gumuz.

The forest crops whose leaves are gathered by Gumuz women for food include *kakima (*which the non Gumuz in the area commonly call *kima)* and *Obosea* (cabbage). *Kakima* is used mainly for making sauce for porridge and they also use the leaves called *okra* for this purpose. So is *tiba* leave, which in most cases is intercropped with maize. *Tsepotiwa* (leave of pumpkin) is also used for the purpose of making sauce. In most cases Gumuz women crop *kakima* in their courtyards and it is a crop, which grows throughout the year. Intercropping such crops with grain is an exclusive task of women in the society.

As it has been discussed above, women use different leaves and boil them during a labour party. The two major leaves to be served on such occasions are o*bosea* and *tiba. Sina* leaves are boiled and served with porridge. Some of the fruits gathered include *deqomsa, ansissa, huya, boha, kuya, qahe,* and*andada*. Unlike the root crops and the leaves, in some cases young boys and men participate in the collection of the wild fruits. However, men and young boys collect such fruits during herding cattle and while they go to bushes for hunting.

The Gumuz employ two different methods of honey collection: wild honey (collecting honey from trunks of trees and caves) and honey production in court yard. In this case it is men who are involved in the different stages like climbing a tree, smoking and collecting the honey. Such a wild honey collection is mostly done in groups the high seasons for wild honey collection being October and November.

The other method of honey collection is using traditional beehives. In the two study villages most of the Gumuz households own two to three traditional beehives. Men make such traditional beehives by using bamboo tree and other local materials. The contribution of women in the construction of the beehives is related to the task of plastering with mud or dung and putting it in the sun until it gets dry. The contribution of women in such method of honey production is also related to the time of transporting the beehives to the tress where they will be hanged. This is always an activity to be performed by women.

The responsibility of men is to hang the beehives on tree where as women actively participate during the collection of honey by carrying the products home. The responsibility of women in honey production extends further to its exchange. In most cases the Gumuz do not consume honey they rather mainly produce it for market. Women are the ones carrying it to the market for selling. Thus the contribution of women in the honey production as in the other supplementary livelihood activities is significant.

LIVESTOCK PRODUCTION

The Gumuz own a small number of livestock mainly cattle, goats, and donkeys. The smaller number of cattle according to informants is related to the absence of plough agriculture. And informants have mentioned that the prevalence of tsetse fly highly risks the task of cattle rearing. They consider animal husbandry as something they were willy-nilly engaged in.

The main purpose of owning oxen among the Gumuz is to the purpose of paying the bride wealth in the absence of a girl to be used in exchange. The other purpose of owning cattle is for the consumption of meat and for sacrificing them during different rituals. Chickens and goats have more spiritual value in rituals. The Gumuz do not use milk and milk products due to the food taboos attached to these products. The degree of rearing cattle for the social values of bride wealth payment and as sacrifice to rituals is more than the economic value to be obtained by selling livestock. The rearing of cattle for market value among the Gumuz is almost non-existent. Goats are the livestock with the largest population at the study villages.

Livestock production is mainly considered to be that of men and young boys. Men in the society are thus the ones who have a right of disposing the dairy products. In most cases raising chicken is considered to be a domain of women. The explanation given by informants for this is that women spend most of their time around home and thus they will have time to feed and water the chicken. The other reason my male informant at Dabasa village provided is that chicken have lower economic value and the task of rearing them requires little knowledge of rearing cattle which requires more knowledge of choosing the grazing land to that and where to take them for watering. Though women are the ones responsible for the task of raising chicken, they have a very limited right of disposing the chickens and their products.

MARKETING

As it has been discussed above the Gumuz base their living mainly on integral shifting agriculture where they employ simple hand tools for production. As a result in most cases what they produce is mainly used for subsistence and it is not meant much for the market. The Gumuz gain most of their income from selling livestock at the market. However, in addition to the livestock sometimes they sell part of their products on a small scale to buy some basic items. Thus the local market exchange has a lower value of income generating for the household. Grains like sorghum, finger millet, and maize are taken to the market.

Oil crops like sesame and Niger seed are produced mainly for exchange. They also sell some domestic animals like goats and chicken. The exchange item women in the study villages often carry to Dibatie, Addis Alam and Ayer Marafia markets is fire wood. By selling these items they buy such essentials as onion, salt, ornaments, edible oil and kerosene. It is the Gumuz women who carry the marketable items to the market with the exception of driving cattle to the market, which is the responsibility of men. The other common trend is that in cases where the items to be carried to the market have more economic values like oil crops men accompany their wives to the market to bargain on the price and to keep the money which is relatively more than the income to be earned from the grains.

Selling handicraft products like baskets and floor mats are also some ways of generating income. Women's market participation is mainly linked to the value of goods and their participation in the market is limited to the less valued items. Men are the ones to decide over ways of spending money obtained from the trade and they also decide the type and amount of grain to be carried to the market.

There is a village level trade in the study villages. It involves exchange of such commodities like handicrafts. Sometimes they exchange salt, oil and grains though it is on a lower scale. The other commodity exchanged on the larger scale is exchange of chicken. This is mainly due to the food taboo attached to chicken where women are forbidden to eat chickens reared in their own home. Women thus exchange chickens with their neighbors and use the exchanged chicken for consumption as the taboo is attached to those raised in one's own home. Informants point out that they also exchange commodities with their neighbors when one is in need of it. Women are the ones who are actively engaged in the village level trade.

Other than the local market exchange discussed above the Gumuz employ different methods of income earning activities. For instance, women among the Gumuz brew local liquor(*araqe*) for supplementing income to the family. The activities performed by women as a supplementary income earning activities include such tasks as vendouring locally prepared alcohol and selling firewood. Two of my informants at Dabasa village explained that they carry firewood to the market at Dibatie town, which is located at twelve kilometers distance from the village. They sell the firewood at 10-12 *birr* on average. They further mentioned that in occasions when they are running out of grains to be used for household consumption, they tend to carry the firewood to markets at Dibatie, Ayer marafia and Addis Alam. The income to be earned from such activity is very low used only to meet needs of families.

REPRODUCTIVE ROLES OF WOMEN

Ellis (1988) defines the three predominant categories of reproductive roles as biological reproductive role, generational reproductive roles and daily reproductive roles. To have a clear image of the contribution of Gumuz women in these activities, the role of women in each activity will be dealt in details. The reproductive role as in the other communities, undertaken by the Gumuz women includes not only biological reproduction but also the care and maintenance of the work force (male partner and working children) and the future work force (infants and children). Besides it involves also caring for youth and old people, looking after the health of household members. Among the Gumuz society, women are more involved than men in the reproductive role as to be addressed below.

THE THREE CATEGORIES OF THE REPRODUCTIVE ROLES.

The generational reproductive roles according to Ellis (1988) include activities such as child socialization, education and guiding activities. As it has been addressed in detail under chapter four women are the ones responsible for raising children among the Gumuz society as elsewhere.

Women spend time with their children and they are the ones responsible in socializing children of both sexes at early ages. In most cases it is following circumcision of young boys that fathers start getting involved in the task of socializing their young boys. Educating young girls in the reproductive roles, orienting them about some traditional practices and taboos, teaching them their future duties as a wife are some of the generational reproductive roles carried out by Gumuz mothers. Women also play a significant role in molding young boys at their early age. They guide their children on how to perform some activities and they advise their children.

The biological reproductive role described by Ellis (1988) deals with the task of child bearing. It involves the activities of child bearing and feeding infants. The discussion of the reproductive role involves childbearing and rearing responsibilities, and domestic tasks done by women, which are required to guarantee the maintenance and reproduction of the labour force. As mentioned earlier the Gumuz attach much value to having children. These activities as Moser (1998) indicates are mostly considered as being natural to women. Similarly the Gumuz believe that the biological and generational reproductive roles are natural to women and it is only them who should feed, care for, and socialize children. The Gumuz consider these tasks as exclusive roles of women and the domains, which are reserved naturally for women.

The third category of the role of reproduction involves the activities performed on a daily basis such as cooking, cleaning and grinding. It was found that, cross culturally, the gender division of labour in reproductive activities tends to be homogenous. In most societies, women are responsible for domestic work, household maintenance and childcare (Mead, 1950; Mair, 1965; Beattie, 1964).

In the daily reproductive chores in the Gumuz society, young Gumuz girls are expected to help with all domestic chores such as caring for younger siblings, carrying very heavy loads of firewood and fetching water, doing agricultural work and food processing. Women shoulder the heaviest burden in household work, including firewood and water collection. Cleaning the house is another activity performed exclusively by young girls and women in the society. Besides they are the ones responsible for cleaning household utensils, washing the cloth of the family and stitching up cloths. All activities like grinding grain, caring for children and sick members of the family, brewing *kiya*, cleaning the house are mainly the activities of women. The *kiya* to be served to children has to be fresh and women have to prepare it two to three times a week. So brewing *kiya* is the most labor and time consuming job on which a woman has to work almost every day. These household activities have to be performed in the agricultural season, which doubles the burden. Women and young girls in the society spend a total of thirteen to fifteen hours working on the daily reproductive activities. This work pattern continues in a woman's life until her old age. Such activities are taken among the Gumuz as natural duties of women.

The task of food preparation starts with the early stage of collecting grain from the granaries to be used for consumption. As mentioned earlier the granaries in most cases are located away from home and women carry some grain to be used for the consumption of one week. They make the grain ready for grinding by freeing it from impurities. The grinding is done by hand using a grinding stone as there is no grinding mill in the villages. They have to collect firewood, and fetch water they will be using for cooking. These complimentary activities make the task of cooking time and labour consuming. The following case highlights the general contribution of women at domestic levels.

Yobiyu Chubat is a woman from Dibisariya clan. She is thirty-two and has five children, (three boys and two girls). I have spent a day to see her -routines. She woke up early to prepare breakfast to the family. She has to grind grain every morning, which she used to make either inga (porridge) or bread. The grain to be grinded in the morning is only the amount to be used for the breakfast. Having served it to her husband and children she dines later. She usually goes to the river, which is located at a distance of about forty minutes from the village, to which she has to walk for about an hour and half. She is the one responsible to clean the house, collect firewood and grind grain for supper and for kiya. As her daughters are too young to help their mother (ages five and three) all these and more responsibilities of the household activities are Yobiyus' tasks. She explains that the heavy workload on Gumuz women is due to the activities related to brewing kiya every day. It takes a total of five days to get the kiya fermented and she uses it only for two days and has to keep on processing the brewing for the next days. She performs most of these activities carrying her three-month son on her back. On a market day she carries the items to the market. She is the one responsible for the task of caring for her children.

The summary below gives a clear image of a day in the life of a Gumuz woman recorded during the harvesting season during the second trip. to *Lay Moga* village in February 2005.

In Gumuz society girls of five to nine years contribute more than twice as much as boys of the same age in terms of the household chores and childcare and continue to contribute significantly more than men throughout their lives. They start to help their over burdened mothers at an very early age. Young boys rarely take care of their younger siblings while it is a common phenomenon to see young Gumuz girls carrying their younger siblings.

A day in the life of a Gumuz woman

Activities performed	Time required for performing the activity
Waking up and cleaning	6:00am – 6:15am
Grinding grain for breakfast	6:15am – 7:10am
Making fire, cooking and serving breakfast	7:10am – 8:45am
Going to the river and fetching water	8:45am – 10:15am
Cleaning the house and dishes	10:15am – 10:50am
Collecting fire wood	10:50am – 12:00am
Going to the field and working on farm	12:15am – 2:45pm
raveling back to the house	2:45pm – 3:20pm
Grinding grain for *kiya* and dinner	3:30pm – 4:45pm
Fetching water for dinner and for the next morning	4:45pm – 6:25pm
Cooking dinner	6:45pm – 8:00pm
Serving dinner and dining	8:05pm – 8:45pm
Preparing dough for the next weeks *kiyya*	8:45pm – 9:15pm
Stitching her sons and her husbands shirts	9:15pm – 10:00pm
Cleaning the dishes, cooking utensils,	10:00pm – 10:50pm
Going to bed	11:00pm

Source: authors field note on February 28, 2005

GENDER AND COMMUNITY POLITICS

According to Mosser (1993), the community-managing role refers to voluntary activities at community level to ensure the provision and maintenance of collective resources and infrastructures (e.g. water points, roads, and health services). Gumuz women are very much involved in this role. This they explain is because deficient public goods and services affect them in the first place. Yet, they often have less access to decision-making than men even when working with men on such issues. One good example of the contribution of Gumuz women in such community managing roles is the active role they are playing being a member of water committee in *Lay* Moga village, where an international NGO (CPAR) is working on a project for supplying a water base. One of my key informants, a woman from *Dibis-ariya* clan, is an active member of the committee. She explains that as it is women who travel over long distances to carry water, they have to be the ones who support the project and work hard for accomplishing it. The explanation of women committee members was that such projects empower them more and they were the ones to benefit much from the project.

Moser (1993) explains the other community role as a community political role. The second category of such activities undertaken primarily by men at the community level is organizing at the formal political level, often within the framework of national politics. These are usually paid works, either directly or indirectly, through status or power. Such activities include political and advocacy activities at community, local, national and international levels, within traditional structures like village headship, party politics, conflict resolution activities and civil society. Moser (1993) explains that such roles are in most cases dominated by men. In the case of the Gumuz society, this role is involvement in local politics and administrative tasks in different capacities as in *gots* and *kebele* is a domain reserved exclusively for men in the society. For instance, in the case of the two study villages, there are no women serving the community at the *kebele* and *got*. According to the information I obtained from an informant who is working in the district agricultural office, all the officials at Angtok *kebele* and the three *gots* are all men. Within traditional structure, among the Gumuz society at the study village's men are the ones who play greater role in conflict resolution activities, in facilitating marriage agreements, performing rituals and in managing household activities. Elders in the community carry out the traditional conflict resolution method widely practiced by the Gumuz (Meron 2010). Women might participate to watch the whole process but they are not allowed to make suggestions unless they are involved to give their testimony

CHAPTER 6

THE GUMUZ WOMEN'S ACCESS TO RESOURCES AND DECISION MAKING POWER

WOMEN'S ACCESS TO RESOURCES: LAND

The Gumuz are patriarchal society who reckon their descent through their father's line, and where patrilocal type of residence remains to be the rule. The common land tenure pattern among the Gumuz at the study area is a one based on communal use right, where a land is apportioned between clan members. Clan members residing in the same clan territory have right of clearing and using a land as long as a certain clan member does not own the land. Such ownership right is reserved for men.

Young boys gain land in such communal land owning system as a gift from their fathers. At an early age of about fifteen young boys would be entitled with the right to claim ownership right of the land. The right of giving, or initiating young boys to own land, is mainly due to the fact that, at that age they are considered to be ready to establish a family. Once gaining such lands, the boys start working hard and using the money they obtain by selling what they produce on the land. They also use part of the money to buy cattle. The justifications given for denying such ownership rights of owning land to young girls in the society are basically two. The first reason is related to the patriarchal type of residence mentioned above. They highlight the fact that young girls would be leaving their natal village on marriage which makes them "an outsider", belonging to their husbands in agnatic lineage. Thus such anomalous social identity of women belonging to their father's clan until the time of their marriage is said to be the underlying factor for the denial of ownership right to young girls and women in the society. The second factor raised during the discussions belongs to the common belief that women and young girls being less competent in skills of managing and owning property.

Besides the ownership rights of land, they are further denied the inheritance right of land and other properties. The common pattern of inheritance among the Gumuz as in most patriarchal societies is primogeniture one where the oldest son in a family will have a right of inheriting land and managing the overall productive activities. Even in the absence of a male heir, the right of inheritance remains to be that of his brother. This in a way facilitates a levirate marriage to be discussed in the following chapter. Women in the society neither have a right to claim ownership and inheritance right to land even on the death of their husbands nor does young girls in the society on the death of their fathers. In polygamous family, when the father dies, the inheritance right is reserved for the first son of the senior wife. Even on the absence of a male heir from the two wives the right of inheriting the property will be given to the person who will be inheriting the senior wife.

ACCESS TO LIVESTOCK

The livestock domesticated by the Gumuz include cattle, goats , sheep, and donkeys (on small scale). The livestock have such social values as bride wealth payment, for men and young boys who do not have sisters to use for exchange purpose use this as an option. Girls do not have right to claim ownership right to livestock obtained as their bride wealth payment on marriage. It is the girl's parents who benefits from the livestock as to be discussed in chapter seven. As in the case of land inheritance right, the right of inheriting livestock is reserved for the first-born boy in the family. In addition to such inheritance right boys in the society have another way of obtaining livestock where they will be using the money they gain by selling the crops they harvested on the piece of land they gained from their fathers. Women in the society as with the case of young girls are denied access to livestock and their products.

The justifications given for their disempowerment in ownership rights to these resources relates to the two dimensional reasoning given above; the incompetence of women and their moving out of the society at times of marriage. It is men who decide on this issue when the need for sacrificing chickens for rituals arise and when the need for selling comes. Women in the society have a right of exchanging the chickens, as it is a taboo to eat chickens reared around home. Their rights to livestock is thus reserved to this right of exchanging the chicken with their neighbors for consumption and the right of deciding on the sale, use for other social purposes like rituals is that of men in the society.

ACCESS TO EDUCATION

Rights and access to resources goes beyond such resources as land and cattle to other resources like education. Though the overall access to education as mentioned in chapter four is a minimum one in the society, the male are the ones who enjoy access to education. One of the reasons raised by the society as to why girls are denied such rights is related to the departure of girls from their natal village upon marriage. Thus it is considered unworthy to invest in "an outsider" as it is believed that her husband's clansmen will be the ones benefiting from girls education than her own parents.

Besides, they have a strong sense of male being the ones who are capable of managing different affairs in the society and that they are the ones who need to education to build their capacity further and to acquire some basic knowledge along that line. Furthermore, there are additional reasons as threat of abduction, which are said to contribute on some scale. The other reason for their denial of access to education discussed under chapter four is the fact that sending them to school is believed to keep them away from helping their mothers at home in addition to the belief that it will keep them away from acquiring some knowledge on how to be an ideal wife.

The main reason for women's denial of access to resources is due to the fact that women move away from their families upon marriage while men stay at home with their wives and continue to contribute to the family economy. Boys are therefore more highly valued, and more investment is made in their education, health, and future income earning potential.

DECISION MAKING POWER OF WOMEN IN THE SOCIETY

In the different productive activities mentioned above, men are the ones organizing the required labor force at the household and village labor commune. They are the ones having a say over when and how to organize a labor force for production. They are the ones believed to have knowledge of when to perform different activities and when the need for such labor input arises, they organize the labor force at home and at the neighborhood for work. Even at those activities, which are said to be exclusive roles of women in the society, it is men who make the arrangements for their wives and daughters. The arrangement starts with setting the day for performing the different activities. It is men who organize women's labor in such occasions as transporting goods to the market. According to informants the only activities where the control of men over women's labor is minimal or non-existent is on the domestic activities. The reason they mentioned is that checking on women's performance on different home chores is an act taken by the Gumuz to underplay the status of men in the society. So in one way or the other men always have the right to organize women's labor when the situation demands. On this point of deciding over her own fruits of labor, Boserup (1970: 50) on the other hand argues "The women are hard working and have only a limited right of support from their husbands, but they often enjoy considerable freedom of movement and some economic independence from the sell of their own crops". However this argument as it has been discussed the ethnographic data does not hold true for the Gumuz.

However, in the case of the Gumuz, a right of disposing fruits of their labor is also that of men. As it has been discussed women among the Gumuz play a very significant role in the hoe based agricultural production activities participating at all levels of productive activities. However, they have a limited access to dispose the products of their hard work. Most of the production is meant for consumption, and in some small scale agricultural production women are the ones to make the best out of the gains, which they use for cooking. Their right over such small amount of products goes to the extent that they tend to sell a small amount of the product to buy basic essentials for cooking like salt, pepper, oil, kerosene, etc. Especially in cases where they are products meant for market men takeover the responsibilities of managing it.

Despite the fact that women equally contribute in the production of market oriented crops, men have more say over disposing such products. For instance, men manage the income earned from selling the oilseeds like sesame. These oilseeds are mainly produced for sale. In cases where these items are taken to the market for exchange, men accompany their wives to the market. Men in the society are the ones having a right of controlling the price and ways of expenditure.

Men informants explained that the difference in decision making is related mainly to the fact that men are the ones who are experienced on such matters and they have the knowledge while women are only good at managing the household chores. Women also agree on this view.

CHAPTER 7

MARRIAGE AMONG THE GUMUZ

The Gumuz have exogamous marriage system, where a person marries out of his clan. Residence after marriage is verilocal, girls have to leave their parents' place and move to their husbands place after marriage. A girl's main role in society is to be a wife and mother, then it may be felt that the sooner to marry her off and let her achieve recognition in the community in this capacity the better it is. In this chapter the different types of marriage, ways of mate selection method and issue of polygamy among the society will be addressed in detail.

THE DIFFERENT TYPES OF MARRIAGE

There are five types of marriage practiced by the Gumuz in the study area. These are: sister exchange marriage (*magilma, angiya*), marriage by bride wealth payment (*bicza*), levirate marriage (*mekola gafa*), marriage by abduction (*datsoko*), and elopement (*mesaqua daguna*).

SISTER EXCHANGE MARRIAGE (*manjielma, angiya*)

Marriage by sister exchange is the most common type of marriage among the Gumuz. Waldeselassie (2002: 71) explains this point in the following manner: "sister exchange (*angiya*) is the most dominant and standard form of marriage". In this type of marriage brothers and close male relatives in a family exchange their sisters or young female relatives with a girl for marriage from another clan. Besides, fathers also use their daughters for the same purpose of exchange for another wife. Fathers and brothers are the ones to decide over girl's marriage. In some cases paternal uncles and their sons can use girls for exchange. The two grooms are the ones arranging the exchange marriage.

The Gumuz consider this as the best type of marriage and which is historical which has been practiced by their forefathers for centuries and which they have to keep on practicing and passing onto their generations. Elders from *Dabasa* clan explain that beside the contract of marriage between the couples married under this system, it secures peace between the clans exchanging girls and it has durability than other types of marriage. They further explain that this is the only type of marriage, which was practiced by their forefathers. Similarly James (1986: 133) contends,"Exchange marriage is a long standing contractual relationship which should last a full generation and is fulfilled by the plentiful birth and survival of children on either side. Many adjustments may be made during the life of such a contract".

In such type of marriage the right of mate selection is exclusively that of young boys and men. They look for their future wives on different occasions like wedding parties, at the market places, etc. The mate selection is done in two ways. The first case is where a boy selects his future wife himself and the other is where his parents make the choice. The first type is the most dominant form. After choosing the girls they inform their parents who play a great role of facilitating the marriage and the exchange of girls. First, parents of the boy check for some basic issues like the skill of the girl, her family background whether her parents are from the caste groups as a *gecenga* (evil eye) or not. Having clarified these matters his parents send elders to the girls' parents.

On the first day of the elders visit to the girl's place, there are some beliefs attached to some of the things they face on their way believed to be either signs of success or failure of the planned marriage. For instance, meeting a person-carrying hoe for digging a graveyard on their way to the girls place is considered as a bad luck symbolizing the death of one of the couples soon after the exchange. Coming across a person washing his body is symbolized as the couples future destitution and hardships. Besides, finding the gate of the girl's parent close on their arrival is said to symbolize the infertility of the girl. On the other hand, seeing monkeys on their way which is believed to mark the fertility of the bride and finding out that the girl menstruating on their arrival. Similarly it is believed to be good signs of fertility of the wife.

On the first day of their visit elders inform them about the purpose of their presence and her parents ask them to take time and they similarly enquire about the the boys' family background. On the second day they make an appointment in order to arrange for the couples to see each other. After such a visit the following event will be exchanging the girls.

On the day of the wedding, a feast is prepared by the bride's parents. On this occasion elders and people at the vicinity will be gathered. On the day of the exchange, young girls will be decorated as it is on occasion when men from the boy's clan look for girls. The bride's best friend will take her to a river and wash her body. She will decorate the bride with *gifqa*, she will put on bracelets (*shihiwliya).* Her best friend will go to a nearby river and collect *gifqa.* Young girls in the village grind and mix it with a seed called *qosa*, to make it sticky when put on the hair and body. Similarly young unmarried girls attending such a party will decorate their bodies in similar manner.

The food and drink prepared will be served to guests at her natal village. Elders of the clan will advise the girl to become a good wife, to respect her parent in laws, not to commit adultery and to respect others. On this occasion her mother and women at the neighborhood will advise the girl to be hard working and to obey her husband and his clansmen and they will also tell her their experiences. Elders and her parents give her their blessings to be fertile and to have a successful future.

Two elders and her paternal uncle together with her best friend accompany the bride to the place of exchange. They usually make such exchange near a river or stream. Up on the arrival of the girl at her husbands' village there will be singing and dancing by his clan members. She will stay in her husband's house and she refrains herself from eating the food and drinking *kiya* prepared by her mother in -laws or on her utensils. She will not be eating from their place until *makorcima* ceremony is held. *Makorcima* is the occasion when the bride cooks for the first time. On this occasion she prepares and serves *kiya* and *inga* to her in-laws and to elders at the village. Young married girls try their best to prepare a delicious food and to brew a *kiya*. The bride keeps on refraining from eating food from her mother in-laws until her mother in-law prepares a feast which is believed to mark that the boy's parents have welcomed the girl to their family. After such a ceremony the girl will be attending rituals, performing productive activities and she starts eating and drinking what her inlaws prepare. This is because it is considered a taboo and she has to use the food and drink she carried from her parents place.

Girls are exchanged after their first menstruation. However, there is an exception to this case. Girls are given as compensation to death in hostilities. In such a case the clan of the killer has to give a girl to that of the slain. The brother of the slain marries a girl given in exchange, if the killer is from a different clan. If it happened to be from the same clan, girls obtained, as compensation will be used for exchange. In such type of arrangement, waiting for the first menstruation of a girl is not a must. In most cases young girls aged eight to ten will be given in marriage. The case of Awgaw's family highlights the points discussed above.

Awgaw is from Dibudiya clan. He died eight years ago. His two sons Abebe and Yasmi are the ones who took over the task of managing the family on the death of their father. Abebe exchanged his sister Emet for his wife Ebawan from Dibishwua clan. His younger brother Yasmi used Erad who was fourteen when exchanged with Echinga from Dibikidwa clan. The boys were the ones who arranged the marriage for themselves and that of their sister. Both Erad and Emet were very young when they were exchanged. The only point in the marriage was that Abebe and Yasmi were old enough to have their wives and that their sisters have their first menstruation. In Abebes' word "If they are young enough to give birth to children, it is alright to give them to marriage. This has been the case with our mother and also it is the same with the girl (Emet)". I remember Emet crying a lot when she was told that she is about to get married. This is a common pattern and it was not because she was very young for marriage". After Erad and Emet left to their husbands place, Nanaish who is the youngest girl to the family stayed with her mother. Her brother Abebe killed a man from Disiwila clan. Elders penalized him by making him pay 1000 birr, as Nanish was too young, only seven, to be given as compensation. Abebe did not have that amount of money. He had to borrow some money from a man from Dibishwua clan. The agreement reached between the two parties was that Abebe will pay the money back within a year. However, Abebe could not pay back his debt within the time of the agreement. The only way of repaying the debt was by giving his sister Nanish, who was only eight by then. Nanish was very young girl for exchange marriage. Abebe often in his discussion mentions that he is lucky to have sisters.

Virginity (*etamaha*) is respected by the Gumuz. They owe respect to girls and in such cases her husband's mother will give her gifts, which in most cases are household utensils like cooking pots and containers for brewing *kiya*. Berihun (2004) describes the case among the Gumuz at Mandura *wereda* as that on the third day after the wedding young and adult men from the village of the bride's family visit the bride and it is on this occasion that they get informed about her virginity. If she was found out to be virgin they will take her to her parents place and they will celebrate the event.

In exchange marriage if one of the women exchanged for marriage is found out to be barren, her husband has the right to ask her clansmen for a replacement. The failure or divorce of one of the marriages through exchange marriage perpetuates that of the other. In such a complex case, the barren woman's parents will give him another girl. If they do not have a daughter they borrow her from a relative, which they will promise to pay back. Girls borrowed from relatives for the purpose of such an exchange marriage are called *Fanjala*. In cases where such a debt between relatives happened due to taking a girl for marriage, the repayment will sometimes exceed to the next generation, where her daughter will be given to her mother's clan. Their grand daughter in such a case will be seen as exchange for her mother and she will herself be used for future exchange.

If a woman exchanged for marriage dies before giving birth, her parents will be forced to give another one as a replacement. The one to be given in exchange under such circumstances is called *hirba*. But if a woman died after giving birth to a child, they are not forced to do such a repayment. Female informants explained that they favor sister exchange marriage than the other types of marriage. Informants explain that the other types of marriage, especially marriage by bride wealth payment, shows low respect to women and women married through such type of marriage are considered as "slave".

MARRIAGE BY BRIDE WEALTH PAYMENT (*Bicza*)

As it has been discussed in chapter three Boserup (1970) and Goody (1976) explain that marriage by bride wealth payment is the rule in African shifting cultivating societies where women perform most of the activities. Similarly, Moore (1988) explains that in African patriarchal society, marriage by bride wealth payment is the common type of marriage. The Gumuz are patriarchal African society where women participate in all the agricultural activities. However, unlike the generalizations made above, among the Gumuz bride wealth is not the common form of marriage. But rather it is the sister exchange marriage which is more wide spread.

In most cases those members of the society who do not have a sister to use for exchange marriage practice marriage by bride wealth payment. Informants explained that in a family where there are few or no female children, fathers start encouraging their boys to farm on their own at early age as a way of accumulating property to be given as a bride wealth payment. The other factor where marriage by bride wealth payment happens is when the girl's parents are in debt and in cases where they want to have money to repay their debts. In such cases, parents tend to give their girls to marriage and they will facilitate the marriage.

There is no standard amount of bride wealth payment among the Gumuz. The amount varies from one clan to the other. For instance, Waldeselassie (2002) lists the amount and composition of the bride wealth among the Gumuz at Mandura as ten cattle, ten goats or sheep, two guns, fifty bullets, hundred birr, ten spears, ten salt bars, and a meqenet (a strip of cloth to be tied around the waist of the bride's mother). Informants at the study villages have described the amount as: twelve cattle, one gun, fourteen goats, three hundred *birr*, ten chicken, five bars of salt, and ten bullets. It is the girl's father who negotiates on the amount of the bride wealth to be paid while mothers have any say on it. Informants point out that though there is no standard measurement, the amount of bride wealth payment in the area has increased, which ten years ago was limited to a two heads of cattle and two bars of salt.

Informants explained that parents of the girl keep the payment than spending it until their girl gives birth to her first child. This is because, in case their daughter happened to be barren, they will be forced t to repay the bride wealth spent on their daughter. If they failed to repay his money in such instances, they would be forced to give a girl in exchange for the barren one. Unlike the case of marriage through sister exchange, in this case the barren woman is considered as his personal property with no attached obligations of returning her to her parents place. They do not consume the meat of the cattle, goats and chicken given by their son in law. This is considered as a taboo and thus they exchange it or sell and buy another one for consumption. As it has been discussed above once a girl is given in marriage through bride wealth payment she is considered as a property to the husband clan through out her life.

The other point in this type of marriage among the Gumuz is that a person who does not have neither the mentioned amount of money for paying bride wealth and nor a sister to use for exchange marriage, can marry a divorced woman and a girl from very poor family by paying low amount of bride wealth. Thus the determinant factors of the amount of bride wealth among the Gumuz include: the economic status of the girl's parent, the marital status of the female to get married, and on the economic status of the person to marry the girl. Marriage by bride wealth payment is less favored by Gumuz women; for they take it as a way of "enslavement" and that a man paying the bride wealth pays it to the labor and fertility of the woman in which case they will be facing a sexual abuse and labor exploitation.

MARRIAGE BY ABDUCTION (*Datsoko*)

Marriage by abduction happens for three major cases. First if a person does not have a sister to exchange in marriage. The second reason is if he does not have enough amount of money to pay as a bride wealth payment he tends to abduct the girl. The third factor is in a case where a person fails to get the approval of the girl's parents. According to informants the third one is a very rare case. In all the three cases the man abducts the girl at a conducive place and time and he will be allying with his friends or brothers for the abduction.

Abduction is one of the major factors contributing for inter-clan conflicts. Abduction is considered as an act of underplaying the status and prestige of the girl's clan. In cases of abduction elders from the boy's clan will be sent out to the girl's clan to request for reconcialtion. The elders decide on the amount the abductor has to pay as compensation for the girl's parents. In the study area the amount is one cattle, two goats, and one hundred *birr*. Besides, he will promise to give his first daughter in exchange for her mother or he will borrow a girl from his close relatives and give her to the girl's clan.

Abduction is one reason that is said to keep parents away from sending their girls to school. An arranged marriage as a compensation for abduction is one factor accounting for the early marriage of young girls. Unlike the bride wealth payment, the girl's parents do not use the money and the cattle obtained as compensation to abduction. This is because of the common understanding in the community that it is equated with bribing oneself for material obtained from a person who has disrespected the family. Men of the girl's clan only use the girl to be given as compensation for exchange.

ELOPEMENT ((*Mesaqua Daguna*)

In most instances of elopement unlike abduction, the married couples usually have earlier affairs. Lack of money for bride wealth payment is also said to be part of the reason but not necessarily the case with elopement as it is with abduction. This might be happening in those cases where the couples rather prefer to use the money to be spent on bride wealth. This is the common trend among the relatively educated couples. As in the case of abduction, this is also considered as an act underplaying the prestige of the girl's clan. Unlike the case of abduction, elopements causes lower degree of interclan conflict. A conflict only happens in cases where the boy fails to send elders to the girl's parents asking for excuse. Like abduction, in this case, the boys groups have to give a girl to the girls group or will promise to give the first born girl.

MARRIAGE BY INHERITANCE (*Mekola Gafa*)

Levirate marriage, the inheritance of widowed women by her husband's brother or close male relatives is a common practice. In most cases unmarried brothers of her deceased husband inherit a woman. Part of the reason for such a pattern of levirate marriage is the security and well being of the children if there are any. It is believed that if the person from her husband's kinsmen inherits a woman he will care for the children and he feels responsible for caring for the children who are also his kin member. A woman has to stay in the family where it is believed that she should continue giving birth to children. A person inheriting a woman has full right over the woman and her children. For instance, he can use her daughters for exchange marriage either for himself and he can also give them to close relatives who want to use them for exchange. The other reason given by informants is exchange marriage is a lifetime contract, where a woman joining a group of people stays giving her reproductive and productive roles throughout her tie unless the relationship end up in divorce, which is a very rare case. Even in those cases when she did not give birth to children her husband kinsmen will inherit her as the divorce of one marriage perpetuates that of the other.

The inheritance has to wait until the *tazkar (the memorial feast)* for the deassesed is held. In most cases it is the brother who is going to inherit the widow that is responsible to prepare the feast. This is the time when it is believed that the mourning of the woman for her dead husband comes to an end. It is the elders who decide over who shall inherit the widow. If the deceased person has more than one wife, they will be shared between his brothers and in such cases, where he has no brother his close male relatives will be given the right of inheritance. In a family where there is a successful hunter, he will be the one to be offered such a right irrespective of his age and marital status. There are also cases where boys inherit their stepmothers.

There are few instances here by the issue of inheritance at times causes conflict between those interested in inheriting the widowed. Besides the care for the children, men inheriting widows are interested in having more children of themselves. They are less interested in inheriting aged widows. The case of Yatinkis elaborates this point.

Yatinkis is a forty-nine years old woman from yagadiwyu clan. On the death of her husband, his younger brother inherited her. She had five children at the time her husband died. The reason for the inheritance was to have someone who can care for her children and to control the land. However, the man left Yatinkis and married another woman as she was in menopause and she could not give birth to children. As of his departure, Yatinkis sons started helping her on the farm activities and she started caring for her children on her own.

POLYGAMY (CHIFA) AMONG THE GUMUZ

As it came out in the discussion under chapter three different scholars have proposed different factors as causes for the practice of polygamy. Of these factors the desire for progeny and labor of women are said to be the major factors accounting for the practice among the shifting cultivating societies in Africa. Boserup (1970) and Goody (1976) explain these as the major factors. Netting (1968) similarly explains that in such African community where women contribute labor on a larger scale, the driving factor is the need to have more labor in production. Gumuz women are engaged on a larger scale in the major livelihood activity, shifting cultivation and in the supplementary income generating activities to the family.

As it came out in the discussion with informants at different occasions, two major factors are said to be the main pushing factors to polygamy. The first factor deals with the productive role of women. Men tend to marry more wives in order to have additional labor force A man needs to have more wives to have more labor force in production. The phrase *indanqua gaf chinka dufayeish* often came up in the discussions with informants, which means that a man having more wives will be of better economic position.

The second factor deals with the advantage of the reproductive role of women, exclusively their biological reproductive role. Men want to have more children, which are considered as social and economic assets by the Gumuz at large. With the second reason informants also explains that the interest of having children is one factor leading to the practice of polygamy. Having more wives has economic implication in increasing the size of one's farmland to be used for more production. The Gumuz explain the importance of polygamy as follows: *indaqua gafa chinka, diduma chinka*, which means a man who has a number of wives will have higher chances of having a number of children.

Wives among the Gumuz often push their husbands to marry more wives. Boserup's explanation is part of the reasons for polygamy among the Gumuz: "Where wives are supposed both to provide food for the family – or a larger part of it – and to perform the usual domestic duties for the husband, a wife will naturally welcome one or more wives to share with them the burden of daily work" (Boserup 1970: 43). Beside her argument for the need for help, they also look for younger wives who can have some children to their husbands. Such a pattern of pushing husbands to extra marriage is a common case with aged wives, who need extra labour force and who cannot give birth to children. Even in cases where women do not encourage their husbands to marry, men take it as they have to get a young and more reproductive and productive wives. Thus the reproductive and productive roles of women are the factors accounting for the polygamous marriage.

Child sex preference is another factor which accounts for polygamy. For instance, if a man has children only of the same sex, he tends to marry another wife with an attempt of getting a child with other sex as it is believed that if women give more than three children of the same sex there are higher chances of producing another one. An additional reason for polygamy among the Gumuz is fertility (Wake, 1977). Incases where a woman is found out to be barren men tend to marry another fertile wife. As it has been discussed among the Gumuz, men have the right to request for the exchange of such infertile wives. But in some cases where the first infertile woman prefers staying with her husband men bring in another woman, which is a replacement to the barren one.

Among the Gumuz another factor that is contributing to the existence of polygamy is the practice of the sister exchange marriage. This is said to be a contributing factor because in a family where the number of sons is lower than a number of daughters, young boys tend to use two or more of their sisters in a way of getting wives in exchange. The number of sisters he has or the number of his relatives he can use for exchange purpose determines the number of wives a man can have.

The other contributing factor for the practice among the Gumuz is the existence of levirate marriage. Even in those cases where the brother of the deceased is a married man, he tends to inherit his fathers wife than giving the chance to other members of his kinsmen. Thus the major reasons for the existence of polygamy among the Gumuz can be generalized under four major factors. These are: the economic factor where by men tend to marry more young wives who are strong to perform productive activities, the need of having more children which have an economic and social value, the existence of sister exchange marriage which allows men to exchange their sisters for marriage as men can marry as long as they can produce male gamete, and the existence of levirate marriage is another factor accounting for the existence of polygamy among the Gumuz at the study area.

THE STATUS AND ROLE OF CO WIVES AMONG THE GUMUZ

The co wives share the same house until the junior wife gives birth to her first child. They have their own beds in the same house and they also will have some utensils of their own. The junior wife (*mahat gafa*) respects the senior wife (*wubtish gafa*) as she has already given birth to some children, which is a status marker in the society.

The senior wives are the ones who can make decision on different affairs at the household level. They are given large amount of land than the junior ones. The justification for this is that they are the ones having larger number of children and more responsibility of feeding their children. Husbands also consult the senior wife on different issues, as they are believed to be matured and have a good experience. The junior wives have no say and they do not intervene and comment on issues that the couples (the husband and the senior wife) discuss about.

The co-wives help each other while working on their respective farms. However the help of the junior wives is more significant as they are the ones with lower amount of land requiring lower labour input. Being a senior wife in polygynous marriage among the Gumuz secures a better status of women among co-wives in a given household. Even in those cases where a junior wife happened to have her own house and farm the size of both the farm and the houses is smaller. Similarly Boserup explains the status differentiation between co-wives in African polygamous family, "the status of the younger wife is inferior as befits the assistant or even servant to the first wife" (1970: 45). In a household shared by the co-wives, the junior wife performs most of the household activities like cooking, fetching water, collecting fire wood, cleaning, grinding grain, while the senior wife in most cases performs the cooking and caring for her children. Senior wives are the ones supervising all the household activities and they are the ones controlling them. The following is a case of a young girl in *Lay Moga* village

Case X was married to her husband a few months ago. She explained that she is still staying with the senior wife. She has a feeling that the senior wife is the one dictating her what to do and not to do. "The senior wife tells me that she is more experienced than me and I am worth to be her daughter. However, she does not consider me as her daughter but she does not even feel that I get tired of working on all the tasks she tells me to do. She let me perform all the activities. I was told by my parents back home to respect her and be peaceful. I have to accept the word of my parents. I wish I have my own farm and start living on my own".

Even in those cases where a woman is allowed to have a farmland before giving birth, during her stay with the senior wife, she keeps her grain in the senior wife's storage, and the senior wife will be the one deciding the amount to be used.

Of the factors causing conflict among the co-wives, the frequent visit of the husband to only one of the wives is the outstanding one. The arrangement of spending the night with the co wives is made in such a way that he spends one *gabaya* (week) with each of them. Besides, he has also to take a turn to help them on the activities on the farm. Informants explained that if the resentment between the co-wives went to the extent that they cannot live together, husbands would construct new house to the junior wife even before having a child though giving birth to the first child is a precondition for constructing new house to the junior wives. But this is a very rare case. The other cause for resentment between co wives is that if one felt that the other is trying to win her husbands attention by different ways like providing him with better food.

The status difference is also indicated in such cases as the privilege the senior wife has in selecting wife for her husband if he tends to marry the third wife. Such a privilege extends to right of inheritance. On the death of a husband having two or more wives, the right of inheriting the land and property is given to the first sons of the senior wives. There is an age difference between the co wives and the husband. In most cases the age of husbands and the senior wives are close while there is a wide gap between the junior wife, her husband and the senior wife. Due to these factors girls among the Gumuz prefer being a senior wife.

Yagako Wale is a woman from Dachiya clan. She was married to Shibabaw Geneti who is from Dabasa clan. They were married in 1985EC. Yagako has five children, four boys and a girl. Yagako owns a farmland of about two hectares. As she does not have a daughter young enough to help her on the farm work and the housework, she initiated her husband to marry another wife:" I forced him to bring another young girl to help me on the farm and household work. I also wanted him to bring another wife to have girls (daughters), which my children will be using for exchanging a wife with, as /birth Missa did not allow me to have more daughters. I wanted to have a young girl who can give birth to a female". Shibabaw decided to marry another wife with the initiation of Yagako. The reasons Shibabaw raised are mainly two: that he wanted to have more children and to have some leisure time getting additional help on the farm work. He married his second wife yazebi umusuya from Dibishwua clan in 1995EC. Yazebi moved to the house of Shibabaw and Yagako after her marriage. Yazebi moved to their place, as it is the rule for her to spend some time with the couples until she gives birth to her first child. In Shibabaw house there are two beds. The one on the right side is that of Yagako, while yazebi has a small bed on the left side of the fireplace. Yazebi narrates the division of labour between her and Yagako as:" I am the one who is performing most of the activities. I fetch water every morning, grind grain and cook breakfast, serve it to the children and us (three of them), I grind the grain for kiya and I make the kiya my self. This is mainly because Yagako has been doing these activities alone for a long time and now it is my turn to help her.

I have to respect her, as she is older than me. On the time I go out to collect firewood and fetch water Yagako will be doing the cooking and caring for children. I have been doing these activities since I came to this place. I am barren and by the time I give birth to a child I will have my own farmland and house. I am barren and now Yagako is pushing Shibabaw to marry another wife. Besides his friends and kinsmen are also urging to do so. He is also in desperation and I have to wait and see my fate".

Male and senior wives favor polygyny. This is due to the advantages they both hope to find by bringing a second wife to the house. On the contrary, girls among the Gumuz do not prefer to be a junior wife. The reason they give for this include some of the facts mentioned above like the burden of working on farm and at the household, the lower access to resources and decision making.

CONCLUSION

There is a generalized assumption on the correlation between agricultural technology, gender role in production, marriage pattern, type of marriage payment and gender-based access to resources. According to Boserup's (1960) and Goody's (1976) argument in hoe based agriculture, it is said that women are the major role players in the task of production.

The explanation given by Boserup (1970) for such pattern of gender division of labor is the use of simple hand tools, which she mentioned are relatively requiring less labor. The involvement of men is limited to such tasks requiring relatively more labor as the first stage of clearing the land, and harvesting.

At this point Boserup's argument converges with the anthropological theory of the gender based division of labor, Strength theory, which states that men always performing arduous activities while women perform simple tasks. The stated correlation between the agricultural technology and gender role in production is not a case among the Gumuz society. The case is slightly different in that both sexes participate in the task of agricultural production. Among the Gumuz the participation of men is not limited to clearing the land. They participate at different activities like sowing, clearing, weeding, harvesting and threshing. Unlike the premises of Strength Theory and Boserup's argument of the involvement of women in the activities requiring less labour, women in the society are considered as having more strength than men being expected to perform those activities which are believed to be arduous. Thus women are always the ones to be involved in activities that require labor such as transporting goods and carrying heavy loads long distance to the market. The famous saying among the Gumuz: *gafa dida anga alma dawit, Gunza anga achinangu* literally meaning women are the ones having the strength of performing activities than men, often comes when the question why do women always perform tasks of transporting and carrying heavy loads? So the answer to this question from the ethnographic data highly challenges the correlation model advanced by Boserup and Goody.

Women among the Gumuz participate in all stages of the farming activity either directly by contributing a labor or indirectly by providing food and drinks for those participating in the labor commune. There are some activities in the agricultural production among the Gumuz that are considered as exclusive domains of men and women. For instance, such activities of transporting seeds to the farm, transporting harvested crops to the granaries are considered as exclusive roles of women in the society, where as sowing and threshing are considered exclusive roles of men in the society.

Women in most cases perform double activities where they are expected to perform the activities and to prepare *kiya* to those participating in the labor force. Their participation in weeding is a conditional one that depends on the size of the farm where they participate in large sized farms.

Thus, the negative correlation between the degree of labour requirement and the scale of women's participation in the production process does not hold true in the case of the Gumuz society. Besides, the central idea of the Strength theory which states that men participate in activities requiring more labour while women perform simple activities does not apply for the Gumuz. Furthermore, though women in the society do not participate in the tasks of clearing and harvesting which Boserup (1970) mentioned as a common pattern among African shifting cultivating societies, they make indirect labor contribution in preparing food and drinks to those participating in the labor commune. Other factors like socialization, raised by Newman (1997), Kahler (1995) and Tiger (1969) shape the gender based division of labor among the Gumuz society. In Gumuz society, while men and women work to the same degree during the peak or harvest period, women work is predominant in the off-season. Men's activities is mostly performed only once in a long time (construction of dwelling units, thatching huts and granaries, participating in hoeing, sowing, harvesting and threshing). In contrast, women's labor input is constant throughout the year, encompassing a wide range of labor-intensive, often tedious, tasks.

Women play a very important and active role in the subsidiary livelihood activities such as fishing, honey collection, marketing and informal income earning activities women do not participate in the wild honey collection, which is exclusively men's domain. However in the second method of honey production where they use traditional beehives for the purpose of honey collection, women are in charge of plastering the beehives made by men, getting it dried and transporting it to the tree where it will be hanged.

Women's role in marketing mainly deals with transporting the exchange items to the market place, where as, men are responsible for pricing them. Women are also active in the village level barter trade where neighboring people exchange commodities. To subsidize income of the family, men participate in the production of handicrafts and women in the task of vendouring local drinks. Animal husbandry is another subsidiary livelihood activity of the Gumuz society. They rear mainly cattle, donkey, goats and sheep and domestic fowls. The domestic fowls are in most cases reared by women unlike the other cattle's which are the properties of men in the society.

The contribution of women in both the biological and generational reproductive roles are significant. The tasks of child bearing and rearing are mainly that of women. Women are the ones performing all the activities of food processing involving the complimentary activities as collecting firewood, grinding grains fetching water and cooking for members of the family. Most of the tasks women perform are complementary in nature.

The role of women in community politics is lower in comparison to their role in productive and reproductive activities. Men are the ones believed to be skilled enough to run local politics, where they are considered to have the knowledge on working at different capacities at *kebele* and *got* level. In some cases of conflict resolution the role of women in the society is in most cases limited to witnessing an event only on the absence of male to witness it. Besides, they are also kept away from performing some activities like participation in the community politics, as they are considered 'immature'. In addition there are gender disaggregated food taboos prohibiting women from eating some foods. The other lower social position of women in the society can be inferred from the way men tend to command the agricultural labour. The anomalous social identity of women belonging to their father's clan up to marriage is said to be the underlying factor for the denial of ownership right to young girls and women in the society.

While drawing the correlation between type of marriage and agricultural technology both Boserup (1970) and Goody (1976) discuss that in African shifting cultivation system marriage through bride wealth payment is the rule. Among the Gumuz shifting cultivating society, the case is quiet different in the sense that the type of marriage mentioned is rather optional than being the rule. The dominant type of marriage among the Gumuz is sister exchange marriage which is considered as the standard form of marriage. It is only on the absence of girls to be used for exchange marriage that a man has to pay bride wealth to the parent's of his will be wife.

Parents, girls to be given in marriage, and men in the society do not favor bride wealth payment which otherwise has been described as being the rule among the shifting cultivating societies. The reasons are parents take it as being indebted in such instances as the dissolution of the marriage due to the sterility of their daughters. Girls in the society also prefer exchange marriage than that of bride wealth payment because once paid to their parents and the girls moved to their husband's place, they have to stay there for the rest of their lives even in the situations where they face hardships and disagreement with their husbands. They take the bride wealth payment as a way of enslaving them. On the other hand men also relate the demerit of such type of marriage with the amount of gifts in money and in kind that they are expected to pay.

The Gumuz favor sister exchange marriage mainly due to the fact that it is one way of securing peace between different clans, as the marriage is clan exogamy. Thus the societal value of women in the exchange marriage system is very significant due to the fact that girls are given in marriage as a compensation for a crime committed. Even young girls are given in marriage as a payment to debt in a society.

Polygamy is a common practice among the Gumuz. The explanation given by Boserup (1970) and Goody (1976) among the shifting cultivating societies is mainly related to the fact that having more wives is meant to have more labour for production. Besides, they also reason it out as to be related to progeny. The Gumuz have more reasons as the existence of sister exchange marriage which allows a man to marry many wives depending on the number of his sisters. Besides the existence of levirate marriage is another contributing factor for the existence of polygamy. Among the Gumuz in addition to the labour factor social prestige to be obtained through having more children is highly valued.

The socioeconomic status of women in the society can be addressed on such variables as: how much importance society confers on females versus males, how much power and authority men and women have relative to each other, what kinds of rights women and men possess, the gender stratification with respect to an unequal distribution of rewards (socially valued resources, power, prestige, and personal freedom) between men and women, reflecting their different positions in social hierarchy. Women in Gumuz society have little or no access to land and other productive resources. Besides, they experience myriad forms of other deprivations such as longer working days, much lower rate of literacy and low level of education relative to men. Customs and traditions are among the factors limiting their ability to access livelihood resources.

In the case of the Gumuz there is no correlation between pattern of women's role in production, their rights of owning and disposing fruits of their labour, and freedom of movement, which has been described by Boserup (1970). Gumuz women have a limited right to own and use grains, like sorghum and finger millet, which are mainly meant for consumption and have lower market values. As the market value of the crops in production increases, the right of women to own and dispose them decreases. This elaborates the low socio economic status they have in the community. Boserup (1970) explains the case of women in African shifting cultivating societies where she says women enjoy considerable freedom of movement and economic independence from the sell of their crops. This generalized assumption does not hold true for the Gumuz, where women's movement is highly controlled by men who also control the labour of women in the society.

Women are disempowered in their access to ownership and decision making rights of different resources. Customs and traditions are among the factors limiting their ability to access livelihood resources. The land holding system in the study area is communal, where men can own land in their clan's territory. In such cases women are denied these rights in their agnatic lineages mainly due to the fact that they are taken as an outsider who will be leaving their birthplaces on marriage. Besides the inheritance right is primogeniture one which is reserved to male children. On the absence of male heir it will be a man inheriting the widow who will be having the right of owning the deceased's property and full right over his children. Women are denied access to owning livestock and men are the ones responsible for the task of rearing livestock mainly; cattle, donkey and goat. Women are responsible for tasks of rearing chickens. The other resource to which women and girls in the society are denied is their access to education. The justification given for such a denial is mainly related to the explanation that girls leave their agnatic lineages place on marriage, which makes it unworthy to invest in their education. Other reasons are an existing belief that considers sending young girls to school will keep them away from learning the household activities. Besides, the probability of abduction is another factor that is believed to keep girls away from education.

Among the Gumuz gender construction starts at early age. This is manifested in such acts as allowing young boys to go out of home, spend some time in bushes, to meet and talk with elders. Young girls on the other hand are socialized to learn the domestic tasks and spend most of their time helping their mothers with the household activities. There are initiation ceremonies for both sexes at the early ages. Circumcision for young boys and menstruation for young girls in the society marks the rite of passage. Gumuz mothers deliver outside of their house. This is mainly due to the fact that they are considered unclean and filthy and due to the fact that dropping blood at home calls for anger of *Missa*.

Such generalized models of Boserup (1970) and Goody (1976) which highlighted the correlation between the existing modes of production – the shifting cultivation – of African communities and the resulting socio economic empowerment of women, is a model that does not hold true for the case of the Gumuz, and perhaps other societies that are organized along similar social organizational principles.

BIBLIOGRAPHY

Abdusamad Ahmed. 1989. "Hunting in Gojjam: The Case of Metekel 1902-32" in Tadesse Beyene (ed) *Proceedings of the Eight International Conference in Ethiopia*, vol, 1.Addis Ababa.

Abeyya Iffa. 2002. "Adaptation, Culture and Changing Environment: The case of the Gumuz of the Didhessa valley (Kamashi zone west Ethiopia)." Addis Ababa University. MA thesis in sociology and social anthropology.

Almaz Eshete. 1991. "Women in Ethiopia: Problems and Prospects". Paper presented at the Seminar on Gender Issues in Ethiopia, Institute of Development Research, Addis Ababa University.

Amott, Teressa and Matthei Julian. 1991. *Race Gender and Work: A multi-Cultural economic History of Women in United States*. USA: South end Press.

Andromeda Tefera. 1986. *The Role and Status of Ethiopia Women*. Washington: University of Howard.

Beattie, John. 1964. Other*Cultures: Aims Methods and Achievements in Social Anthropology*. Cohen and West Ltd.

Bender, L. (1973). *The Ethiopian Nilo-Saharans*. Addis Ababa: Artistic printers.

Berihun Mebratie. 1996. "Spontaneous settlement and Inter-Ethnic Relationship in Metekel: North West Ethiopia". MA thesis: social Anthropology, AAU.

—. 2004. *The Past in the Present: The Dynamics of Identity and Otherness among the Gumuz of Ethiopia*. Trondheim: Norwegian University of Science and Technology (NUNU).

Bernal, Victoria. 1988. "Losing Ground-Women and Agriculture on Sudan's Irrigated Schemes: Lessons from a Blue Nile Village". In Davison(ed). *Agriculture, Women and Land: The African Experience*. London: West View. Pp. 131-157

Bonvillan, Nancy. 1995. *Women and Men: Cultural Constructs of Gender.*. New Jersey: Prentice-Hall, Inc

Bossen, Laurel. 1989 "Women and Economic Institutions" in Plattenr(ed) *Economic Anthropology*. Stanford: Stanford University Press. Pp. 318-350.

Bohhanan Paul. 1968. *Tiv Economy*. London: Longmans.

Boserup, Ester. 1970. *Women's Role in Economic Development*. New York: St. Martin's Press.

—. 1990. *Economic and Demographic Relationships in Development*. London: The John Hopkins press Ltd.

Bryson, Jean. 1981. "Women and Agriculture in Sub-Saharan" In Nici Nelson(ed). *African Women in Development Process*. London: Frank Cass and Company Ltd. Pp. 29-46

Bryceson, Deborah. 1995. 'African women Hoe Cultivators: Speculative Origins and Enigmas" in Deborah F Bryceson (Ed) *women Wielding the Hoe: lessons from Rural Africa For Feminist Theory and Development practice*. Oxford and Washington, DC: Berg Publishers.

Central Statistical Authority. 1996. *The 1994 Population and Housing Census of Ethiopia: Results of Benishangul- Gumuz Region*, Volume I Statistical Report, Addis Ababa.

Ceruli, Ernesto. 1956. *People of south Western Ethiopia and its Borderlands*. London: International African Institute.

Chodorow, Nancy. 2001 "Family Structure and Feminine Personality." In *Feminism in the study of Religion,* edited by Juschka, Dm London: Continuum.

Chaftez, Janet. 1989. "Gender Equality: Toward a Theory of Change", in Wallace, R. A. (ed) *Feminism and Sociological Theory.* .London: SAGE Publications. Pp. 135-160.

CPAR. 2000. "Situational Analysis and Baseline Information: Benishangul Gumuz National Regional State, Dibatie *Wereda*". Dibatie.

Damie Wayessa. 1980. "The Dikeria and Deosega of lower Didhessa valley of Western Wallega." BA thesis in history. AAU.

Daniel Haile. 1979. "Law and Status of Women in Ethiopia". Addis Ababa: African Training Center for Women, Economic Commission for Africa.

Davison, Jean. 1988 . . . "Lands and Women's Agricultural Production: The Context". In Davison(ed). *Agriculture, Women, and Land: The African Experience.* London: West View. Pp. 1-32.

Dejene Aredo. 1989. "The Gender division of labour in Ethiopian Agriculture: A study of time allocation among people in private and cooperative farms in two villages". Department of Economics, Addis Ababa University.

Desalagn Rahmeto, 1988. "Rural Women and Household Labour Use patterns in Ethiopia: A review of some evidences". *Paper presented for the tenth International Conference of Ethiopian Studies*. Paris.

—. 1990.Rural Women in Ethiopia: problems and Prospects. In: Tsehai Berhane Selassie, ed. *Gender Issues in Ethiopia*. Institute of Ethiopian Studies, Addis Ababa University. Pp. 47-54.

Di Leonardo, Micaela.1991. *Gender at the Crossroads of Knowledge: Feminist Anthropology in the Postmodern Era.* Berkeley: University of California,.

Dixon Muller. 1989. *Women's Work in Third World Agriculture*. ILO: Geneva.

Ellis Frank. 1988. *Peasant Economics: farm Households and Agrarian Development.* Cambridge: Cambridge university Press.

Kessing, Roger. 1981. *Cultural Anthropology Comparative Perspective*. New York: Holt, Rinehart and Winston.

Edossa Tassisa. 1982. "The Gombo Shanqilla of lower Didhessa valley and the campaigns of Abba Tonie, 1952". BA thesis in history. AAU.

Emiru Kenea. 1984. "The Khaza of Ebantu to 1936".BA thesis in history, AAU.

Evans-Pritchard, Edward. 1951. *Kinship and marriage among the Nuer*. Oxford: Cladendon Press.

FAO. 1986. "Population and the labour force in rural economies". *FAO economic and social development paper*. Roma. No 59,

Gottlieb, Alma and Thomas Buckley. 1988. *Blood Magic: The Anthropology of Menstruation*. California: University of California press.

Guyer, Jane. 1984. "Women in the Rural Economy: Comparative Variations." In Hay and Sticher (eds) *African Women: South of the Sahara*. London: Longman. Pp. 19-32.

Goody, Jack. 1976. *Production and Reproduction: A comparative Study of the Domestic Domain*. Cambridge: Cambridge University Press.

Hanna Kebede 1990. "Gender Relations in Mobilizing Human Resources" in seigfried Pausewang, et al(eds) *Ethiopia: Rural Development Options*. London: Zed books.

Hirut Terefe 1997. "Gender and Cross-Cultural Dynamics in Ethiopia with Particular Reference to Property Rights, and the Role and Social Status of Women". In: K. Fukui, et al., eds. *Ethiopia in Broader Perspective: Proceedings of the 13th International Conference of Ethiopian Studies*. Kyoto: Shokado Booksellers. Vol. 3: pp. 541-561.

Irwin, Lee.1968. "Some Notes on Say Say Culture". In *the Journal of Ethiopian Studies*.Vol. vi, no. 1.

James, Wendy. 1979. *Kwanimpa: The making of the Uduk people: An ethnographic study of survival in Sudan Ethiopian Borderlands*. Clarendon press. Oxford.

—. 1977. "Notes on the Gumuz: Their Culture, history and survival" a paper presented at the conference of Ethiopian Origins at the School of Oriental and African Studies.

—. 1986. "Lifelines: Exchange marriage Among the Gumuz" In Donham, Donald and James (eds).*The Southern Marches of Imperial Ethiopia: Essays in History and Social Anthropology.* Cambridge: Cambridge University Press. Pp. 119-147.

Kahler, Ernest. 1995. *Sociology: an everyday life Approach . . .* St Paul: West Publishing Company.

Keller, B., E. Chola Phiri and M. Milimo. 1990. 'Women and Agricultural Development' in Wood, A. et al. *The Dynamics of Agricultural Policy and Reform in Zambia.* Ames: Iaowa State University Press, Pp. 241-62.

Kessing, Roger. 1981. *Cultural Anthropology: A Contemporary perspective*. New York: Holt, Rinehart and Winston.

Lorber, J and Farrell Susan.1991. *The Social Construction of Gender*. Newbury Par. London: Sage Publications.

Mair, Lucy.1965. *An Introduction to Social Anthropology*. Oxford: Clarendon Press.

McCann, James 1988. "History, Drought and Reproduction: Dynamics of Society and Economics in Northeastern Ethiopia". *In the Ecology of Survival: Case studies from Northeastern African History*, London: Lester Crook.

Martin, King. 1978. *The status of women in Pre Industrial Society*. NewJersy: Princeton University Press.

Melesse Getu. 1995. "Tsamako Women's Roles and Status in Agro-Pastoral production". MA thesis in Social Anthropology. AAU.

Meron Zeleke. 2003. "The Autobiographical Narratives of: *Dajjazmatch* Yemane Gbregziabher, Doctor Haile Walde Masqal, and *Shalaqa* Mossisa Dheressa". BA thesis in History, AAU.

—. 2010. *"Ye shekoch chilot*; traditional institution of Conflict resolution in Ethiopia"; in *the African Journal of Conflict Resolution* (ACCORD).

Minh-ha, Trinh. 1989. *Woman, Native, Other*. Bloomington: Indiana University Press.

Mohiuddin, Yasmeen Niaz.1997. Gender Inequality in Pakistan Labour Market: Myth and Reality. In; Janet M. Rives and Mohammed Yusuf (Eds). *Economic Dimension of Gender Inequality*: A Global Perspective. London: West Port.

Moore, Henrietta. 1988. *Feminism and Anthropology*. Cambridge: Polity Press.

Moser, Carolyn. 1998. *Gender planning and development: Theory, Practice and Training*. London: Rutledge.

Murdock, George. 1960. *Social Structure*. New York: the Macmillan Company.

Nasality, Ruth. 1988. "Women in the Colonial Economy of Bungoma: "Role of Women in Agriculture, 1902-1960". In; Davison(ed). *Agriculture, Women, and Land: The African Experience*. London: West View. Pp. 56-73.

Nelson, Nici. 1981"Introduction" in Nelson(ed) *African Women in Development Process*. London: Frank Cass and Company Ltd. Pp. 1-9.

Netting, Robert. 1968. *Hill Farmers of Nigeria: Cultural Ecology of the Kofyar of the Jos Plateau*. Seattle: University of Washington Press.

Newman, David. 1997. *Sociology; Exploring the Architecture of everyday life*. California: Pine Forge Press.

Njoku, John E. Eberegblulamm. 1980. *The World of African Women*. The Scarecrow press, Inc. London.

Parkin, David. and David, Nyamawaya eds.1987. *Transformation of African Mar-*

riage. International African seminars, No 3. Manchester: Manchester University Press.

Pine, Francis. 1996. "Gender". In Barnard, A and J Spencer, (eds). *Encyclopedia of Social and Cultural Anthropology*. New York: Rutledge, Pp. 253-262.

Plattner, Stuart. 1989. *Economic Anthropology*. Stanford: Stanford University Press.

Ragassa Aboma. 2000. "Gender and Agricultural Production among the Maqi Oromo". MA thesis in Social Anthropology. Addis Ababa.

Rogers, Barbara. 1980. *The Domestication of Women. Discrimination in Developing Societies*. London and New York: Tavistock publications.

Sachs, Carolyn. 1983. *The Invisible Farmers: Women in the agricultural production*. Rowan and Allen held. New Jersey.

—. 1996. *Gender Fields: Rural Women, Agriculture and Environment*. West View Press.

Sandy, Peggy. 1974. "Female Status in the Public Domain", in Rosaldo and Lamphere (eds). *Women, Culture and Society*. California: Stanford University Press. Pp. 189-206.

—. 1981. *Female Power and Male Dominance: On the Origins of Sexual Inequality*. Cambridge: Cambridge University Press.

Sisay Muche. 1988. The Reaction of the Gumuz Towards Resettlement Programme With particular reference to Metema Gumuz settlement. BA thesis Sociology. AAU.

Staudt, Kathleen. 1995. "The Impact of Development Policies on Women" in Margaret J. Hay and Sharon Sticher(eds) *African Women South of the Sahara*. New York: Longman Scientific and Technical.

Susan, Hill Gross and Mary, Hill Rojas. 1990. *Contemporary issues for women south of the Sahara*. Virginia: Polytechnic Institute Press.

Tadesse Tamirat. 1988. Nilo-Saharan Interaction with Neighboring Highlanders: The Case of the Gumuz of Gojjam and Wallega". Institute of Development Research(ed) Proceeding of the Workshop on Famine Experience and Resettlement in Ethiopia. Addis Ababa, AAU.

Tefera Tegene. 1985. Traditional Marriage System of Shanqilla Society of Metekel. BA Thesis in Sociology, AAU.

Tiger, Lionel. 1969. *Men In Groups*. Norwich: Fletcher and Son Ltd.

Tiruneh Zena. 1976. "Economic Characteristics of peasant families in the Awassa area, Chillalo Aweraja". (Assela ARDU publication No 1).

Triulizi, Alessandro. 1986. "Nekemte and Addis Ababa: dilemmas of Provincial Rule" in Donham and James(eds). *The Southern Marches of Imperial Ethiopia*. Cambridge: Cambridge University Press. p. 51

Tsehai Berhaneselassie. 1991. *Gender Issues in Ethiopi a*. Institute of Ethiopian Studies, Addis Ababa University.

United Nations. 1990. *Patterns of First Marriage: Timing and Prevalence*. New York: Department of International Economics and Social Affairs.

Unseth, Peter. 1985. "Gumuz: A Dialect Survey Report". *Journal of Ethiopian Studies*, Volume 18: 91-114.

Wake Staliand.1989.The*Development of Marriage and Kinship*. Chicago: University of Chicago Press

Waldeselassie Abute. 2002. *Gumuz and highland settlers. Differing strategies of livelihood and Ethnic Relation in Metekel, Northwestern Ethiopia*. Guttenberg: University of Guttenberg.

Wallmark, Peter.1981. "The Begga (Gumuz) of Wollega: Agriculture and Subsistence" in: Bender M. I., *Peoples and Cultures of the Ethio-Sudan Borderland*. East Lansing: African Studies Center, Michigan State university. Pp. 79-116.

Weideger, Paula. 1977. *Menstruation and Menopause: the Physiology and psychology, the myth and reality*. New York; Delta press.

Zenebework Tadesse. 1975. "Overview of Ethiopian Women". A paper presented for Seminar on the contemporary role of women in society. Addis Ababa: Ethiopia.

—. 1982. "The Impact of Land Reform: the case of Ethiopia" in Lourdes Beneria(Ed) *Women and Development: The Sexual Division of Labour in Rural Societies*. New York: Praeger.

Zenebework Tadesse and Yared Amare. 2000. *Berchi Journal*, Volume 1, No 1,. "Women's Land Rights in Ethiopia. Pp. 25-53". *Journal of EWLA*.